Nanette V. Hucknall

Finding Your Work, Loving Your Life

A Guide to Help You Discover and Attain Your True Vocation through Practical Higher Self Techniques

SAMUEL WEISER, INC.

York Beach, Maine

First published in 1992 by
Samuel Weiser, Inc.
Box 612
York Beach, ME 03910

Library of Congress Cataloging-in-Publication Data

Hucknall, Nanette V., 1933-
    Finding your work, loving your life: a guide to help you discover
and attain your true vocation through practical higher self
techniques / by Nanette V. Hucknall
        p.   cm.
    1. Work — Miscellanea.   2. Vocation — Miscellanea.   3. Karma.
I. Title.
BJ1498.H83   1992
131 — dc2O   92-20655
                                                                CIP

ISBN 0-87728-749-X
BJ

Printed in the United States of America.

The paper used in this publication meets the minimum requirements of the American National Standard for Perma-
nence of Paper for Printed Library Materials Z39.48-1984.

Dedicated to my guru RHH,
MM, and MA in gratitude

Table of Contents

Acknowledgments

I am grateful for the higher Guidance I received while writing this book. It was the source that inspired and motivated me to do the work. I would also like to thank the following people:

Judy Bach, for her help, encouragement and advice; her being there made all the difference.

Matthew Breuer, for advice about esoteric material; his insights were invaluable.

Sharon Magruder, whose help and belief in me and in the material was a constant reassurance.

Nanette V. Hucknall

Introduction

This book is for you if you are dedicated to the pursuit of your personal goals; if you are concerned about your spiritual growth and how your work can help that growth; or even if you are seeking a deeper understanding of evolution itself. If you already know your life's work but are having problems fulfilling it, there are practical planning and visualization methods to help you work through the difficulties. If you are already working in your chosen field and are experiencing obstacles in achieving success, this book will provide a better understanding of the causes of the obstructions. It will also help you bring goals into focus in your daily life and establish the sound practices that can bring success.

Such success is achieved through working with the transpersonal or higher Self.[1] This Self is the part of the individual that is connected to and in contact with the higher forces of nature. It contains the wisdom of humanity. Within It is the source of the higher knowledge that relates to the cosmic realms. The higher Self is within each and every person, but few are aware of this part of themselves. "This Self is above, and unaffected by, the flow of the mind-stream or by bodily conditions; and the personal conscious self should be consid-

---

[1]The word *Self* is always capitalized to differentiate it from the personal self. Whenever the word *Self* is written, it refers to the higher Self.

ered merely as its reflection, its 'projection' in the field of the personality."[2]

To grow spiritually a person must awaken this part and bring it into his or her consciousness on a regular basis. The Self perceives evolutionary patterns and understands what each individual needs to accomplish to help spiritual growth.

To know the Self is to begin to know your own spirit. This book works with the higher Self by suggesting exercises that will help you awaken and contact it. Through regularly working with the higher Self there will come a deeper awareness of who you are, as well as a better understanding of those around you. The higher Self is you, and all your accomplishments are contained within it.

The higher Self represents a personification of wisdom and is often seen by the individual as an archetypal Wise Being. This figure is generally masculine to both men and women, though it can also appear as feminine. Seeing It personified helps the individual relate to the Self more closely. It is also possible to not see a Being, per se, but to instead see a symbol, or light, or feel energy. In all cases the ultimate goal is to integrate the higher Self into the consciousness so you are working with It at all times.

Throughout this book, the words *vocation* and *life's work* signify broader meanings than their normal usage. In several ways these words connote what in the East is called *dharma*. Dharma has a variety of interpretations in Buddhism and Hinduism. It represents the way we live our lives spiritually and ethically, as well as the way in which we develop on our evolutionary paths.

One of the many meanings of dharma refers to the work a person chooses to do in a given lifetime. This work relates to the individual's evolving soul, which incarnates lifetime after lifetime and carries with it, in each subsequent life, all

---

[2] Roberto Assagioli, M. D., *Psychosynthesis* (New York & London: Penguin Books, 1976), p. 19.

the experiences it has gone through in previous lives — both negative and positive.

The work one selects is very important, as it always helps the soul go onward to another level of maturity. Everyone has to live lifetimes in such fields as the arts, sciences, philosophies, etc., to achieve the experience needed for spiritual balance. For example, if you have lived many lives in the arts, developing right-brain attributes, such as intuition and imagination, then you would need to have a few lives in the arena of the logical, left-brain sciences to bring balance.

The purpose of the evolutionary path is for the soul (or individuality) to achieve synthesis with the higher energies and bring itself to the place of total assimilation into the highest world.[3] The soul then will no longer need to return to Earth, but can continue its evolution in a higher realm.

In the ancient teachings, dharma denotes the entire evolutionary path, including the performance and accomplishment of work. It also signifies religion, natural law, universal order, truth, knowledge, morality and duty. I refer to a Hindu definition in which dharma signifies duties and obligations. In the Bhagavadgītā much emphasis is placed on the need to follow or fulfill one's dharma (social duty or role). "The universe is sustained *dharma*. Ideally each person works out his social career according to the dictates of his own nature *(svadharma)* as this is itself a product of past experience. *Dharma*, *karman* ("action" or "work"), and *samsara* ("rebirth") belong together: action carried over innumerable lives must be informed by a sensitivity to the obligations one has in virtue of one's interdependence with others."[4]

Because dharma includes the hidden influences, both spiritual and psychological, it relates in a much deeper way to

---

[3] Considered the highest state of spiritual bliss — in Buddhism, it is called Nirvana; in Agni Yoga, the Fiery World; in the Kabbala, the Atziluthic or archetypal world; in Christianity, heaven.

[4] Bhagavadgītā, from *The Encyclopedia of Religion* (New York and London: Macmillan and Free Press, 1987), vol. 2, p. 126.

what I mean when defining life's work or vocation. Therefore, as you read this book, be aware that vocation or life's work means the specific work you will be doing, but the work also relates to your spiritual and psychological growth, as well as to your relationships with others.

This book speaks openly about reincarnation and karma. Both terms come from Eastern ideology. For those of you whose culture disclaims the possibility of recurring lifetimes on an ascending evolutionary path, you can translate these terms as impressions, coming from what Jung called the collective unconscious. These impressions can affect your finding and fulfilling your true vocation. It would, therefore, be advisable to substitute *unconscious* when the book talks about recalling the *past* (lifetimes).

1

Using the Higher Self to Find Your Work

If you believe you know or have been doing your life's work[1] and would like to learn more about the best way to accomplish it, then you can begin this book with chapter 2. I would suggest, though, that you devote some extra time to this chapter in order to be certain the work you are doing is truly your vocation and not something you chose because of outside influences. If you selected a particular profession for the wrong reasons — to placate a parent, for example, or for ego gratification — this work may not be your true vocation. The exercises in this chapter will tell you directly if you have, indeed, made the right choice.

For those of you who have thought about life and what it holds for you, but have not decided how you want to spend the rest of your lives, it is important to take as much time as needed to work with these exercises. Maybe you made a decision based on what seemed appealing at the time. Too often the young are misinformed about the kinds of work available and waste years in professions that are boring and unstimulating.

---

[1]The words *life's work* and *vocation* can be used interchangeably. Both refer to the jobs that the incarnating spirit chooses to fulfill in its new life. In this book, these words have a broader meaning than their normal usage. See the Introduction, page xii, for their full definition.

People can have problems discovering their true vocations for various reasons—including ignorance, lack of education in a particular field, and emotional difficulties. For
example, people who have problems with self-acceptance
would have difficulty pursuing any vocation that required
leadership and responsibility. So it is necessary to look into
the inner self to discover the true life's work. Emotional
blocks may exist with roots in this life, or a past life, or both.
These blocks can keep people from discovering their true vocation. Working with the exercises in this book should indicate any deep-seated blocks that need to be understood. The
following case illustrates this.

> Isabel was a 19-year-old woman who came to me for
> help to discover her life's work. She was in college,
> majoring in English, but was totally confused about
> what she wanted to do. Working with her brought
> up interesting images: wild horses running, a fire
> burning, a camera, an airplane, but nothing hap-
> pened when she worked with these images. Finally
> her higher Self showed her a map of South Amer-
> ica. Exploring further, she saw an image of herself
> in the jungle writing a book she thought was per-
> haps about botany or the ecological system.

> We did an imagery session during which Isabel
> imagined going through a typical day in South
> America. At the end of the exercise she placed the
> whole experience in her heart[2] and felt immediately
> that something was wrong. It just didn't feel like the
> right work. We went through a few more imagery
> sessions, changing the work and adding to it, to find
> out if something was missing, but each scenario

---

[2]Throughout the book, when I use the word *heart,* I refer to the heart chakra or
center, sometimes called the heart chalice, which is an energy center located in the
middle of your chest. This center is a direct channel to the higher Self. It is not
connected to the physical heart.

failed to find a response in her heart. Isabel was getting very frustrated and self-critical. Why wasn't she getting it?

In one scene she saw herself in a jeep, chasing a herd of animals on a plain. It didn't develop into anything else, but at the time it didn't seem right to me that it was in South America. I had Isabel go back and relive the scene, and while she was experiencing it, I asked her where she was. She suddenly turned white and started to shake with fear, crying, "No, no, I can't go back there, I can't go back to Africa." Isabel then saw herself as a black man running through the jungle being chased by white men. Her feeling was she was captured and horribly killed by them. This past life experience was completely blocking her from seeing her vocation. Her work was to be in Africa, but the terror of being there again was keeping her from seeing what it was.

Taking some of the images she'd already experienced and placing them in Africa revealed to her that her vocation was to return there and work on the animal preserves. The camera she'd seen earlier indicated that she would keep a photographic record of her work, and the plane would be her means of transportation. When she played this scenario out and placed the experience in her heart, she felt a burst of joy and knew it was right.

Her higher Self, by first showing her images of South America, helped her work through the fears that had blocked her from seeing Africa. Now Isabel is in college majoring in zoology.

When we feel we have successfully accomplished our life's work in a given lifetime, we die with a sense of completion which helps our souls to continue onward along the evolutionary path. If we feel we have failed in our life's work — whether that be true or not — karmically,[3] we need to return to do the work again, not because of what it means in the material world but because of what it means to our evolving souls.[4] At this time on the planet, many people have experienced many different kinds of work in various fields, such as the arts, sciences, politics, etc., This is important for the growth of each soul — to experience all these areas of knowledge, but with a sense of achievement. This does not mean that it's necessary to achieve fame but simply that our souls must feel they have done the best work possible, whether as mail clerks or senators.

Remember, the soul needs to follow its evolutionary course. Any sense of failure will inhibit it and cause a feeling that it cannot succeed, no matter what happens. If we die with these feelings, our souls will be impressed with this sense of failure. This results in feelings of worthlessness in subsequent lifetimes, and these feelings intensify if not corrected.

This is why being happy is very important. It is also important to consider whether your present job is your true vocation. The work doesn't have to lead to fame and fortune. It is more significant that you experience a sense of success in your chosen work. If you feel you have achieved something with your life, that feeling is impressed on your soul and goes forward with you to the next life. Therefore, try to determine what it is you are meant to accomplish and work toward manifesting it in this life.

Discovering Your Life's Work

If you don't know what your true vocation is, the following exercises will help. It is important to work with your higher

---

[3]Karma is the law of cause and effect. Explained more fully in chapter 9.
[4]Soul is the incarnating individuality that contains all the experience acquired from lifetime to lifetime, both positive and negative.

Self on a regular basis. Using these exercises can help you connect with It. After you have used them for a while, you may find it easier to connect with the higher Self and you may then not need to go through each entire exercise but can keep the parts that are helpful to you.

In doing the exercises, be aware that everyone is unique and experiences a visualization differently. Some people can see the scenes in their mind's eye, whereas others will just feel or sense what's happening. There are also people who are auditory, they hear sounds and voices. Some will experience a combination of sensory impressions. Feel free to eliminate or add material to the exercises. What's important is what works for you. Some people may want to tape these exercises so they can listen to the tapes.

Exercise 1

Get comfortable. Close your eyes and feel your whole body relaxing from the tips of your toes all the way up to the top of your head. (pause) Each part of your body is feeling relaxed. (pause) Take some deep breaths and center yourself by linking with your heart center. (pause) With each breath, feel the cares of the day dissolving into nothing. (pause) Now imagine you are walking on a path that leads up a mountain. The path is very gradually leading uphill, so it is easy to walk on. (pause) The sun is shining brightly and you feel its warmth on your body. (pause) The path leads through an evergreen forest, and you experience the trees around you as you climb. Imagine the beauty of the green trees against the blue sky. (pause) You can hear or sense the birds singing in the branches and you listen to the different melodies. (pause) You come to a clearing and imagine, in the distance, the sound of a waterfall. Go off the path to the waterfall and look at or sense the water's rapid descent from the top of the mountain. As it hits the rocks nearby, feel the wet spray on your face. (pause) Continue walking up the path. You are now higher on the mountain with only scrub brush around.

Stop and look, or feel the mountains around you. (pause) You are now near the very top of the mountain. It is flat and there is a bench there. Sit down on the bench and experience the wonderful view. (pause) Directly above you is the sun. Imagine in it a face of a wise and loving Being looking down at you. The face becomes a figure and the figure slides down a sunbeam and sits down next to you on the bench. (pause) It is your higher Self. Sense everything about It. (pause) Link your heart with Its heart. How does it feel? (pause) (If it feels right, you can continue, if it feels wrong, stop the exercise and do it another time.) You can now ask It any question you want. Do this, and listen to Its answer (it can be words or impressions). (pause) Reach over and hold your higher Self's hands. Feel Its energy flowing to you. How does it feel? (pause) Imagine yourself blending into It, so that the two of you become one. (pause) Does It tell you any more about your question? (pause) When you feel ready, open your eyes and write down everything that occurred.

Exercise 2

Sit in a comfortable chair. Close your eyes and relax. Take several deep breaths and, on each exhalation, relax all your muscles. (pause) Put all the cares of the day out of your mind and let them disappear. (pause) Become aware of your heart center, which is in the center of your chest. Feel it as a centering, balance-place for your whole body. (pause) Now imagine yourself standing in the middle of an open meadow. It is a beautiful day, the sun is shining brightly and there is a soft breeze blowing. (pause) Experience the meadow around you — the trees, the green grass with wild flowers growing, and the mountains in the distance. (pause) You can smell the sweetness of the air, feel the warmth of the sun and the gentleness of the breeze blowing against your body. (pause) Suddenly, in the distance, across the meadow a figure appears and slowly walks toward you. You know the figure is your higher Self. As It comes closer, try to sense what It looks like.

(pause) Is It a man or a woman? How is It dressed? Experience It. (pause) The figure will come to a stop in front of you. Link your heart with the heart of the figure. Does it feel right to you? (pause) Imagine the sun's rays surrounding the figure, encompassing It in light. Does It remain the same? (pause) (If it feels right and It stays the same, you can continue, otherwise stop the exercise and do it another time.)

Now that you are facing the figure, you can ask It anything you want. It will answer you, either with words or impressions. Ask your question. (pause) When you feel finished with the dialogue, slowly come closer to your higher Self. (pause) Reach over and hold Its hands and feel Its energy flowing to you. (pause) Imagine yourself blending into your higher Self. (pause) How does this feel? (pause) Does It tell you more about your question? (pause) When you are ready, slowly open your eyes and write down what occurred.

• • •

Choose one of the exercises and once you have connected with the higher Self, ask the following question:

What is my life's work?

You may get a direct answer or just a hint. Write it down, then ask again. Keep doing this, writing everything down, even if it's just an impression or a symbol that seems to make no sense. Don't think about it, just write it down. This process may take several days or weeks. The Self will usually reveal a little at a time. Don't feel rushed. When you reach the point at which you don't receive anything at all, then you know it's time to go on. You will probably have a list of items to work with. If the list is very long, try to group the items into categories, like the arts, the sciences, etc. Then do the following exercise:

Focus your attention on your heart chakra. Take some time to experience the energy that is there.

Then, imagine placing an image of one of the categories in your heart center.

If it is difficult for you, just say to yourself:

"My image of _____ is in my heart," and THINK it there.

Then tell your higher Self:

If my life's work is in this category, please let me feel it in my heart.

The heart chakra responds in various ways. It may start to pulse or move in a circular motion. It could also feel like it is expanding or emitting warmth. Working with it on a regular basis will help you discern what is the right reaction for you.

Pick the category your heart responds to most strongly and work with each item in the group. If initially you didn't need to make categories, take your list of items and work with them the same way. Connect with your higher Self and, one at a time, place the items in your heart, asking the higher Self, *Please show me more about this.*

Take whatever you receive and keep working with it, asking to see more. Do this with each item until you have a larger picture of what your work could be.

● ● ●

If you are working with symbols, follow the same procedure. Place the symbol in your heart and ask to see more about it. A symbol usually represents something of importance, and patience is required to reveal what that is. You can also dialogue with the symbol. Do the following exercise:

Close your eyes, relax. Take some deep breaths, letting go of all your cares. When you feel totally relaxed, visualize the symbol before you. Then place it in your heart, asking it: "What do you mean?"

If you get an answer, take the answer and try to find
out more by continuing the questioning.

Select only those items you have felt strongly in your heart.
At this stage you will probably be working with actual professions. For example, you may feel your work is in the arts, and
you have come up with the profession of being an art director
in advertising or an art gallery manager. The next step would
be to take these jobs and do a separate visualization with each
one:

> *Go through a typical day of work. Imagine doing
> this job and try to experience what that feels like.*
>
> *Experience all the things that could happen.*
>
> *Realize the good parts — what is that like for you?*
>
> *Then see the negative and experience what that is
> like.*
>
> After going through all the pros and cons, take the
> job and place it in your heart center and ask your
> higher Self:
>
> *Is this the work I'm suppose to be doing? Feel the
> response.*

You should have a definite feeling at this stage as to what
your vocation is to be. (If you are not familiar with the job,
try to find someone who knows about it. Ask about a typical
day and what it would be like.)

• • •

If you feel blocked at any time during the process, connecting to your higher Self can help you set aside your fears
and obstacles. Try working in the following manner. At a time

when you are alone and very quiet, link with your higher Self,[5] feel it within you and say:

> *Help me remove my fears so I may understand what*
> *I am meant to accomplish in this life.*

You may want to try doing this with a friend or a group of people. You can help each other. Consciously picture your fear as a round black ball and give it to the other people to hold for a while. Let each person in the group visualize taking the ball from you so you will be free to ask your higher Self to show you what your work is meant to be.

If someone has fears relating to a specific job, this method helps break through those fears. But if the fears are much deeper and relate to having suffered karma from misdeeds in previous lives, then this exercise will not work. In such instances, the individual needs to work on remembering which life or lives caused the fears. This process requires a longer time and, in some cases, requires work with a therapist to uncover the deeper insecurities.

The Importance of
Accepting Your Vocation

One of the fears people have about knowing their true vocations is that they will then be responsible for accomplishing them. But there can be no more excuses. Just look at all the people you know who are unhappy with their work but stay with it because it is the only thing they know how to do.

In many cases these people are afraid of the responsibility of fulfilling their vocations because in past lifetimes they incurred karma that has seriously affected their psyches. As a result, they will often do the opposite of what their work is meant to be. If they are meant to be in positions of authority,

---

[5]See the higher Self exercises, chapter 1, pp. 4-7.

they will take more menial jobs or work alone. If the vocation is to take place at home alone on creative projects, they will usually be found in jobs surrounded by others who constantly make demands on them. The following case illustrates this point.

Steven, a man in his 30s, lived alone in the country, working as a carpenter. He liked his work but always felt something was missing. When he meditated on his life's work, he kept seeing himself in an office, and each time he saw the office it would jolt him out of meditation. The thought of having to work 9 to 5 in an office was repugnant to him.

We first had to work with uncovering his fears. What was it about an office that made him so fearful? He realized it wasn't just being a worker, it was being a manager. The fear was being responsible for directing people. The idea of being in a situation where he was in charge of a group made him break out into a cold sweat and he was immobilized.

I realized Steven's fears must be related to a past life that would have to be revealed if he was to continue. By working with his higher Self, he began to see bits and pieces of a lifetime in which he had been a landowner and ruler of a small province. Finally, one night he had a dream in which he saw himself being overly authoritarian and abusive to his workers. He publicly whipped one man he felt had insulted him. As a result, the man brought about an uprising against him and Steven was captured, horribly tortured and murdered. The fear of being destroyed if he were ever again in a position of authority was extremely strong in his unconscious. Seeing that lifetime helped him understand those fears.

Through working with the higher Self, Steven eventually realized that he needed to be in a responsible position again, in order to have the chance to be a good leader. The fears would certainly be there, so we worked with an affirmation in which he told himself he was capable of being a compassionate and kind person who can be responsible and understanding.

Steven was determined to learn as much as he could about people skills, and that helped him start his new career. He eventually became a manager in a major corporation. And while the need to be controlling still comes up once in a while, because Steven has learned to be conscious of those moments he can stop himself and change the pattern.

For you to know and accept your vocation, you must ask your higher Self to help you uncover it step by step. Each step will reveal a new insight, and each insight, when meditated upon, will bring forth the next step. It is like unraveling a ball of yarn. When all is completely unraveled and laid out, it's then possible to discern the colors and patterns, and understand the best way it is to be knitted. If you resist accepting your vocation, it might take you longer.

Remember, the higher Self always knows the true vocation but cannot reveal it completely if there is any fear about knowing it. The higher Self allows you to work slowly toward discovery, helping as much as it can. In some cases, answers are revealed very quickly. In others, it takes time.

Never feel rushed in finding your life's work. Be sincere, and work at the pace at which you're meant to work. If you are working in a group with this process and are stuck in your fears, ask the group for help.

2

ACCEPTING YOUR VOCATION

The last chapter dealt with ways of getting in touch with your life's work. In this chapter we assume that you have been able to come to an understanding about your work through visualization, and by working with others.

Much of the work you need to do in understanding your true vocation concerns the attitude you have about it. This attitude can either help you fulfill your life's work, or it can impede you. First, it is important to understand why you have a certain vocation to fulfill.

We sometimes accept vocations without questioning why our incarnating spirits have chosen that specific work. Knowing about it does not mean we truly want to do it. In fact, the work may be totally repugnant. People who feel this way will often be conscientious about fulfilling their vocations, even though it is in opposition to their feelings. They need to come to a better understanding of why it is important to do their chosen work, otherwise they will not be happy. The following example illustrates this situation.

> A 25-year-old woman named Laura came to see me. She dabbled in the arts but wasn't sure whether to be a painter, a sculptor, a decorator, or to pursue something new—like performance art. She was hoping that by working with me it would clarify the exact area in which she needed to work.

Since she was very visual, it was easy for her to see her higher Self right away. She saw It as an old Chinese wise man dressed in a red embroidered robe. When she asked him to give her an indication concerning her life's work, he led her to an office that had her name on it. Inside, she saw on the desk some papers with mathematical calculations on them. She became very upset and told her higher Self, "This isn't art. What is this? Show me the art work I'm going to be doing." He shook his head and disappeared.

It took several sessions and some convincing for her to let him show her what he knew, and not what she wanted to see. First, it had to be determined if her life's work was to be an artist. Her wise man took a stick and drew in the sand a picture of her painting, then erased it. He next showed her sculpting and erased that. He then went through each thing pertaining to art, erasing it every time with a shake of his head. Laura felt he had to be wrong, but when she placed being an artist in her heart, there was no response. When she dialogued with this higher Self, he told her, "You were an artist in the past, several times. It's easy for you. That's why you're still attracted to it." He then drew her head and divided her brain to left and right and showed her that the right was developed and the left underdeveloped. What she needed for balance was to develop the logical left brain.

It took a while for her to accept that her work could be in a different field. And it helped when she realized her higher Self wasn't telling her to give up her art completely. She could always do art as a second vocation, and her first vocation would be as enjoyable, if not more so.

When Laura let go of the art, she was able to allow her higher Self to show her exactly what her vocation was. It turned out that her work was to be structural engineering, something very strange for her to even think about. But when she placed it in her heart, she knew it had to be true. The difference in feeling between being an engineer and an artist was too clear for her to doubt any longer.

Laura felt it would be difficult. Going back to school was terrifying, but much to her surprise, she had no difficulty with a subject like calculus. Her success was an affirmation that helped her to continue working toward her goal.

As I explained previously, a specific vocation is chosen according to the spirit's or soul's needs on its evolutionary path. It will require some very deep meditative searching within the self in order to better accept the destined work. This deep inner search is helped by questioning the higher Self. Connect with your higher Self[1] and ask the following questions:

1) Why is it necessary for this specific work to be done in this lifetime?

2) How can I best accept the work? If it is work that you have a hard time accepting, ask: How can I best accept this work when it is something I don't feel particularly drawn to?

3) How can I feel within me a real desire to pursue this particular work?

4) How can I start to pursue my vocation. What is the first step?

---

[1]See the higher Self exercises, chapter 1, pp. 4-7.

All these questions can be answered from within. No one else can give you those answers. The higher Self knows the best way to proceed. To receive correct answers requires patience and a very strong positive attitude. If you come up against resistance and feel negative, that will block the process completely. The attitude should always be very positive, and the best way to achieve such an attitude is to allow yourself to be totally involved in the process itself. Let that process be exciting and stimulating. Be full of curiosity and enthusiasm about finding out about your vocation. It is indeed exciting when you come to the deeper realizations. Believe in them and the belief will help you penetrate through any barriers.

It doesn't matter how long it takes. What is important is to really understand the purpose of your life. How many people have ever truly come to that realization? Very few. So if it takes you weeks or months or even a year or two, it will be well worth the effort. And it is only through this understanding that you can have the enthusiasm to strive to fulfill your vocation. That striving is needed for success. Again, success is defined as doing the work you are meant to do as well as you possibly can.

Also, it is necessary to work in harmony to find contentment and peace within. This peace can only be brought about through a balance of energy. If you are doing your destined work, then your energy is being used in the right way, which helps bring about the balance. In contrast, if you are doing work that is not destined for you, your energy needs to be constantly forced and used in a manner that will put you out of balance.

Through fulfilling your work and achieving a balance of energy, you also affect the people around you. If you have a job, a good exercise is to notice the people you work with. It's easy to see who enjoys their work and who doesn't. Be aware of how both types affect you. Notice the difference, and, most importantly, notice how you affect others. Also watch to see who is the most efficient.

So often there is a struggle within between the part that understands what the work should be and the part that has fears connected with it. This latter part will impede knowledge of the vocation, and even when that knowledge is uncovered, the same part will impede the work being done. It is important when you come to an understanding of your vocation that you are also aware of those parts that are resistant. It cannot be emphasized enough how important it is to work on those resistances. Sometimes it is even better not to consider beginning the work until you've dealt with the resistances. Otherwise, you will not do your best work. The following case represents this situation.

Tom, age 31, was back in school studying biology, with the goal of getting his doctorate and doing research. This was in response to what had slowly emerged from his process of working with his higher Self. He'd had a lot of resistance about going back to school, mainly because he had been a poor student and had, in fact, dropped out of college because he was failing. After a great deal of struggle and a lot of therapy — which helped him to come to terms with his need to fail — Tom was doing very well in school, making good grades.

In his junior year his higher Self began to indicate that he should consider going to medical school to become a doctor. All of Tom's resistances came up, and even though he had an A/B average, when he went to take his entrance exams he did poorly and lost his chance to go to medical school.

During his period of resistance, Tom got in touch with a lifetime in which he had been a doctor. He had been doing research and had developed a vaccine he felt certain would work against a terrible disease of that day. He tested it on a few people, and as part of the test, left another group with no vaccine. When the latter group died and the group that had taken the vaccine were cured, the doctor felt so guilty that when he got the disease himself he allowed himself to die.

Tom is now deeply afraid of becoming a doctor, which, of course, is why he sabotaged his entrance exams. He is presently in graduate school and going for a doctorate degree in biology. Interestingly enough, his school requires that he take some of the medical courses along with the medical students. Those are the courses at which he works hardest and enjoys the most.

To understand your vocation and come to a full acceptance of it, you also need to look at how the work will affect your life. Besides planning how you can best fulfill your vocation, it's important not to forget your personal needs. The work should be in accordance with those needs—needs that may or may not relate to it. If your needs are diametrically opposite to the work, how can you be happy in doing the work? Your emotional and spiritual needs or patterns should be in balance and correspondingly in harmony with the dharmic patterns. This brings about synthesis. To emphasize one without the other is to only allow one aspect of the evolutionary path to be fulfilled.

There are three sets of patterns that need to be brought into harmony. To do so, a deeper understanding of all three is necessary:

The first pattern—the work, itself—requires a deep inner probing of your nature relating to life's experience.

The second pattern—the emotional, psychic needs—relates to the ways in which you relate to others in the material world. This comprises the requirements for love, friendship, companionship—

all the physical and psychological needs carried over from past lives or developed during childhood.

The third — the spiritual pattern — relates solely to the higher subtle world[2] and its divisions. These are the patterns of your spiritual nature that are striving toward the higher realms. If they are awakened, they can pull with or against the others.

It is important that you to recognize these three sets of patterns within, so the following chapters deal specifically with each, in order to help you better understand your own personal makeup.

---

[2]In metaphysics, the seven invisible worlds or plains above the Earth, ranging from the astral to the Fiery World; the *lokas*.

3

HARMONIZING YOUR WORK

Arriving at an understanding of your life's work is the first step toward acceptance. Fully accepting and integrating it into an overall understanding takes several steps. The first is recognition of the work. Then, depending on your personal enthusiasm, the second is planning the best way to accomplish that work.

If there is no desire to do the vocation, then a change of attitude is needed. Some negative feelings could have been caused by your having failed at the same work in a past life. As a result, karma that is difficult to overcome was incurred. To discover if this is the cause of your own contrary attitude, connect with your higher Self[1] and ask:

Please show or let me feel if I have a past life that could be generating resistance to my doing my vocation.

In most cases, the answer will come from an inner knowing. A past life might be seen, or you may simply know that you have done this work before. That knowing will be something felt deep within. If you have developed a lot of intuitive awareness, you can sense whether something is correct or not. When you experience something, place it in your heart center

---

[1]See the higher Self exercises, chapter 1, pp. 4-7.

and feel whether it seems right. The feeling is what counts, and your heart will always tell you whether something is true or not. Practice this with everything, and it will help you accomplish the work ahead.

Also, simply discovering a resistance because of a previous life in which you experienced failure will not alleviate that resistance. In fact, sometimes it becomes even stronger when its cause is understood. You therefore need to look at the resistance and understand all its aspects, as you will see from the following case history.

> Arthur always knew he wanted to be a lawyer. There was never any question in his mind—until he got into law school, when he suddenly found himself unable to study or concentrate. He had been an A/B student in college, so he knew it wasn't his ability that was in question. Arthur really became frightened when he realized he was beginning to fog out during lectures, either not understanding what was being said or completely forgetting.

> In working with him, a past life came up in which he had been a criminal lawyer representing poor thieves in 19th-century England. It was a difficult job, and he lost many to the gallows. He died poor with a sense of not being good enough.

> When Arthur saw this, his reaction was to become discouraged and depressed. He felt it was crazy to become a lawyer again and wanted to quit law school. His resistance was a barrier comprised of all those men and women he felt he had failed—a formidable barrier that he had no desire to overcome.

> I persuaded Arthur to go through the life from beginning to end. Slowly he began to see that there were times when he succeeded in helping people—not just a few but many people. He saw that his

main problem was his feelings about the injustice of the political system of that past time, and his unsuccessful attempts to change it. His courageous efforts had only brought him disgrace in the eyes of his peers, who labeled him a "criminal-lover," a dishonor to his profession. All of that affected his sensitive nature so that when he died, he felt a profound sense of failure.

Now, though, Arthur was finally able to see the positive parts of that life and acknowledge to himself that he really had done a great deal of good. He saw he had been an advocate of truth and not a failure at all! That his feelings of failure were caused by the social pressures he'd had to withstand at the time. It helped him to see that those feelings of lack of worth were preventing him from realizing that he was truly capable of again becoming a good lawyer. He still carries within him a need for justice, so it's no surprise that Arthur became a criminal lawyer. It is important for him to do it again with a sense of having succeeded.

Reaffirming the positive part of a past life can help alleviate fear and resistance. Often one becomes lost in feelings of self-recrimination and self-contempt, failing to see the positive side of the life, but rarely is a life a complete failure. Every life has both positive and negative aspects, and if the soul carries both forward, then the individual should look at both realistically. If the soul does not carry forward the positive aspects, it is because the individual in that life came to a very despicable end, an end in which the soul felt totally desecrated. That type of life brings karmic repercussions, but rarely does one have to repeat it. The lives that could have caused a sense of fear or failure are usually more well-balanced. Often, the individual simply wanted to be perfect. As a consequence, since perfection does not exist in the mundane world, there was a sense of failure, and it is this sense of failure that is carried forward.

If one died as a result of making a mistake or doing something wrong, this also causes the soul to experience a sense of failure and a fear that failure will cause death of consciousness. But this is a misinterpretation of the life experience. What is needed in working with such lives is a broadened understanding of the meaning of perfecting the spirit.

In working with these concepts you need to become far more impersonal in the way you handle perceptions. To perceive yourself in a previous life as having done wrong is to immediately create a block to understanding. Do not judge your past. Just try to understand the experience and see how it relates to you today. Criticizing or judging yourself will only impede comprehension. Awareness develops a deeper realization of what actually happened and what caused the attitude of failure to arise. This helps overcome the resistance.

It is always the deeper reality rather than the bare facts of what happened that needs to be probed. There is a recognition that takes place in the inner nature. Understanding your past helps in acceptance, as long as there is a non-judgmental attitude. If you are full of fear, full of anguish, or full of sadness when probing the past, it is best not to proceed. It is better to accept that there is a deeper grief within that needs to come out one day, but the time is not yet right for that to happen.

Discovering these things within is to discover an unending river containing all the emotions life can hold. If you are ready to let that river flow, it will happen naturally. If, in your probing, you sense or feel something, try to understand it but don't force the feeling if it is too painful to go deeper.

The work that has been chosen for a specific lifetime usually reveals itself at a time when the soul is able to look at the resistances and overcome them. If the time is not ready, do not force it. Realize that when your soul is ready you will come to that understanding. If you see and feel more at this time, also be aware that bringing up some of the past can be a painful experience for the psyche. Be gentle with yourself and remember that each individual on the planet has to experience everything that life offers—the negative as well as the positive. We have all been everything or will be everything in order to come to a realization of the evolving spirit.

You will at a certain point, in working to recognize your vocation, come up against fears, fears that do not necessarily relate to a past lifetime but reflect on who you are in this life. For example, if you are insecure as a person and find that your vocation is to be a leader, your insecurities will flare up and make you feel fearful of doing the work.

Childhood conditioning can cause a feeling of unworthiness that will block and interfere with the pursuit of one's destiny. These types of fears will need to be looked at in a manner that will not only reveal their nature but help alleviate them. The use of psychology can bring better discernment. Depending on the depth of the neurosis, the vocation may have to be put aside for a time until it's possible to overcome the feelings.

Another reason for not doing one's vocation is an attitude about life itself. If there is a fear of doing hard work and a desire to live a life of leisure, then the labor involved in performing the work will not be appealing. Often, the individual will put off doing the work until it is too late. When the attitude is positive, the work will be done.

The attitude of someone striving to help humanity can be derived from two sources. One source is pure intent coming from the spirit. The other can be caused by a motivation based on self-aggrandizement. Outwardly these can look the same, but they are quite different beneath the surface.

Therefore, it is important to become aware of your underlying motivations. If you sense within yourself a need to have power, look at it as it relates to your vocation and understand how you can work with that need in order to not hurt others and to be of service. Awareness is always the key to success. As long as you keep that alive throughout your life, you will be successful.

It is no easy task to look at yourself constantly as through the eyes of an outsider, recognizing your imperfections, as well as your outstanding qualities. But once you have worked with the resistances and fears, and are past them, you can honestly work toward ways of accomplishing your vocation.

4

Your Personality and Your Work

It is important to understand why an individual is supposed to do certain work, and to realize why someone can be born with certain psychological characteristics that can either enhance or obstruct the work. For example, a person given the vocation to become a great leader may come into this life with handicaps that will not only cause psychological disturbances but also impede pursuit of the vocation. Why does this happen? Why are there so many obstructions in certain cases? The cause is complex and relates mainly to the karmic pattern of the individual. A handicap is usually caused by negative karma incurred in a previous life. The ability to overcome the karma, and the handicap, and still do the vocation is also part of the capacity of the person. It is a far greater challenge, but a challenge that can be overcome.

A good example of someone overcoming a tremendous handicap is Franklin Roosevelt, who succeeded in his vocation despite physical impairment. His many fine, courageous qualities enabled him to work through the handicap, illustrating what a positive attitude can accomplish.

Usually, though, when there is a handicap, be it physical or mental, the handicap can prevent someone from successfully pursuing a vocation. To be successful, one must therefore strive to overcome the psychological problems the handicap causes. If the problems are conquered, it will strengthen the soul to move further on the evolutionary path. And overcoming any kind of handicap builds the strength necessary to continue onward and do the work that is destined. The ideal is to balance the vocational pattern with the psychological pattern.

Don't feel discouraged if in pursuing your work you come up against a strong psychological barrier that feels almost impossible to overcome. Dealing with these barriers is always the best way to grow spiritually. They are never impossible to overcome, though it may take time and a great deal of inner work to do so.

Now, to achieve a balance between the psychological pattern and the vocational pattern involves looking carefully within and deciding what is essential for personal growth. Personal growth has to encompass both work and personal needs — needs that relate to the environment and relationships. If those needs are overlooked or buried, you will feel unhappy in the work you choose.

In most cases, it's possible to balance some of these needs in everyday life. But there are instances when pursuing a career can result in total immersion and neglect of those personal needs so important for balance and synthesis within. The person who neglects these needs, though successful in the eyes of the world, will often feel frustration about the personal life, which will affect the soul at death. Even if the life's work has been fulfilled, a sense of incompleteness will be carried forward. So it is very important to come to a true balance within. The following case demonstrates this point.

> John was a workaholic. It started with his first job, just after he was married. He was under a lot of pressure and felt he had to prove himself, so he worked late nearly every night. His wife complained a lot, so he changed jobs.

> The new job was less demanding, but John wanted to make it to the top quickly, so he added more and

more responsibilities to his workload. Naturally, the more he took on, the later he had to work. He didn't dare ask for more help. Soon he was working long hours again. By this time he had a family, and he convinced his wife that he had to make more money to support her and the children.

After his promotion to manager, John found himself with a large staff who took over much of his workload, but he still worked late. His excuse then was that his children were too noisy and he needed some quiet.

I met John when he was in his middle 50s, long after the children were grown. He'd continued to work long hours, though his workload at the time wasn't very heavy. Usually, after 5 o'clock he would make up things to do. Unfortunately, he would also get very annoyed if his staff didn't put in long hours, too, and when they did, their time was mainly spent sitting in his office having long chats.

He really believed he was making huge sacrifices for the company. When I talked with him one time about his family, he finally admitted, "When I go home at night, I haven't much to say to my wife. It's a bit of a strain." Basically, John was a good man who had lost his connection to life and didn't know how to get it back.

The opposite extreme is someone preoccupied by pleasurable, personal relationships. Too often, this type lives for pleasure alone and never completes the vocation. Sometimes the destined work isn't even begun! The need for personal relationships can often be a disguise for fear, preventing the individual from looking seriously inward. Recognition of the fear is extremely important if one is to move forward in a more balanced way.

Also, too much focus on having pleasure can divert one from the life's work, and it can sometimes cause neurosis. Psychologically, the soul needs to release patterns of frustration that cause this type of divergence; sometimes this is done with the help of therapy.

We are discussing various emotional growth patterns. These patterns are tied into past lives and can reflect on the psyche in many different ways. Learning about these patterns is difficult because they are fraught with desire and emotions that may not be understood easily. Deep feelings from within that cause unsettledness or anguish can change a person's outlook and ways of doing things. This type of conditioning is very subtle and often not recognizable.

If, for example, a person feels emotionally unstable from having suffered great losses in a specific lifetime, there will be a sense of sadness, with a great desire for personal love and attachment. Such a need can overwhelmingly change the manner in which a person thinks about doing a vocation. For that individual, only personal relationships will matter. Eventually, understanding emotional patterns will help, but this will not necessarily change the desire. In order to do the vocation without this type of strong interference, it is often necessary that one has the desired relationships first, putting them in their proper perspective. Only then can the vocation be pursued. The following case demonstrates this point.

> Jason was in an unhappy marriage for fifteen years. He felt duty-bound to stay in it because of the children. Eventually, when they grew up, he got a divorce. Jason's only desire was to find the perfect love — he had fantasized for years about what she would be like.

> At the time he had a vocation he needed to pursue, but his desire for the ideal mate became so overwhelming he had to drop everything. Of course, the fantasy was so real that, naturally, no woman he met could come close to fulfilling it.

Jason frequented singles' bars, went to every party, joined all the clubs and even placed ads in a New York magazine. He met many woman, but none matched his fantasy. He went through disappointment after disappointment, irrationally blaming everyone for his fantasy not coming true.

After a great deal of agonizing, Jason had a dream that helped him understand where his fantasy came from. He had been a soldier in his last life. In the dream he saw himself being sent off to World War I with no time to marry the woman he was seeing—a woman he deeply desired with unrelenting longing. He had died in battle with this unrequited desire in his heart. He was today still looking for her, but none of the women he was meeting in this lifetime could match his image of her, which was, of course, blown way out of proportion.

While Jason still has a great need for a companion and has continued to look for her, at least now he will date women who are different from that of his fantasy. But what he seeks now are certain qualities, rather than a lost image.

Everything must be in balance for the soul to feel completion in a particular life. Too much emphasis in one area brings imbalance and frustration. The best way to look at life is to honestly feel within the heart a sense of peace, love, and friendship for oneself and for others. If you can have a feeling of wholeness that reflects the inner spirit, then psychologically you have found that place of synthesis.

Such a state is idealistic in this world, a world that pulls men and women by its strong physical attractions. It is very important to find a relative sense of fulfillment within the personal life, but this is also difficult to find.

It's good to look at the way in which you relate to others. So often people relate to each other without awareness. Step-

ping back and observing your relationships, with the use of
the heart, brings greater understanding and acceptance, and
improves behavior. No relationship is without misunderstand-
ings and differences, but these differences can always be overcome if the individuals respect and accept each other.

The world, itself, needs to work at relating. When two
countries oppose each other in ideology, there often seems to
be no way of reconciliation. If two people from either country can meet and compare human values there can be com-
monality. No matter what a person's background, there can
always be found similarities with other people. The need to
relate is a need we have evolved into. That is why relationships
are important for the human psyche and why the absence of
positive, loving relationships causes unhappiness and neurosis. So this area needs to be worked on simultaneously while
we strive to fulfill our life's work.

Examine your feelings. Are you happy and content personally? If you are not feeling a oneness with your whole self,
then examine in more depth what your personal needs are.
And don't just think about them with the mind. Really examine what your heart cries out, for it is only within the heart
that you can find truth. Look for that truth concerning your
own personal desires and let those desires come into awareness. If the desires are too strong and too impossible to be
reconciled, then you may need to re-examine why the desires
are there in the first place. All of this relates to your personal
happiness. There is nothing wrong in wanting to find happiness. The soul seeks it and longs for it lifetime after lifetime.
Do not then feel unworthy if you seek happiness. Only realize
truly what your personal happiness has to be. It differs for
each of us.

Happiness in your personal life brings inspiration and
creativity to your work. Again, it is attitude that is important.
Don't feel you need happiness all the time, but know that it
should exist in your life more than less.

5

Natural Law and Spiritual Growth

It is very difficult to talk about evolution of the spirit when to most people spirit is an intangible essence. How can something that seems so intangible evolve into anything, especially if the result of this evolution is something equally difficult to discern? To tell you that the spirit comprises many minute particles of matter would also make it hard to understand, since most people think of matter as something they can see and touch.

In the higher subtle worlds, matter can be vaporous. Yet, if that vapor were to be under a highly sensitive microscope, one might discern very tiny particles, particles that under even larger magnification would show patterns containing even further categories of minute matter, matter that has within it highly charged magnetic properties. These properties react to each other in a pattern similar to that of atomic particles.

This reaction, or pattern of attraction, occurs within each individual in its own peculiar manner. When someone experiences a certain type of physical manifestation — for example, breaking a leg — the event impresses a specific molecular arrangement on the pattern of particles. This arrangement remains intact and becomes part of the overall pattern, or what is sometimes called the individuality or soul. Therefore, each experience someone goes through leaves an impression within the actual soul.

When the soul incarnates, the patterns within it form what is sometimes called the subtle body.[1] This invisible body contains all the impressions from previous lifetimes. It is like having thousands of tiny cells which form the subtle body, cells held together by an invisible series of energy streams. These streams are full of properties relating to the higher worlds. If someone is developed spiritually, then the stream of energy comes from one of the higher planes of existence. If an individual has not developed the spirit within, then the subtle body resides mainly in the lower subtle planes. As someone changes through spiritual striving, the streams of energy change in accordance with the spirit. This helps the subtle body rise from one plane to another in the spiritual ascent.

If you have been a high initiate[2] in a past life, you have developed your subtle body such that it can travel to the higher subtle worlds. Even if you have not again achieved the same initiation for several lifetimes, it doesn't matter in terms of the subtle body, which always remains the same, in accordance with the highest spiritual development. For instance, if you achieved a high level in a life a thousand years ago, into every lifetime afterward you were born with the same subtle body. According to your needs, and according to your karma in a particular life, you may or may not use your subtle body to its full potential.

But having a developed subtle body doesn't mean always using it on the subtle planes. If you are going through very emotional times in the physical world, you may not seek to go

---

[1] The subtle body corresponds to the subtle worlds. It has many degrees, but the highest state, which is the mental body, corresponds to the Fiery World. As we develop spiritually, we develop the subtle body, enabling us to go into the higher worlds.

[2] A student of esotericism who has developed spiritually through the trials of each level. The completion of a level is signified by a special initiation given by a sage who is the student's teacher. Each initiation signifies one's having conquered an aspect of the lower nature.

to the higher worlds when sleeping.[3] Instead, the lower emotions will totally envelop the subtle body, keeping it from being released.

The spirit, when it is awakened, directly implants its impression onto the subtle body. This impression in turn awakens a longing for the higher realms of existence. The longing in itself begins to change the patterns of the subtle body. As this longing is followed by the individual's striving, it will change the subtle body, allowing for it to make its ascent into the different higher worlds. As this happens, a reciprocal mechanism starts to operate. As the subtle body changes and is released to go into a higher plane, the energy of that higher plane enters within the body itself and changes the patterns.

This is similar to the alchemy of the ancients when they changed base metals into precious ones, which took place through the induction of higher forms of energy. These higher forms of energy could only be produced by the alchemist's own spirit. If the alchemist had not achieved knowledge of the higher planes, there would be no way he could make the change occur. All true alchemists were, therefore, very high initiates.

To examine the subtle body would be to see many tiny particles floating in a wave of energy that would make them appear very luminous. If one could see it with the eyes, one would see threads of incandescent light surrounded by clusters of shimmering colors, also luminescent. The heart chakra is a vessel lined with billions of crystals of light and energy. To see the subtle body of a high initiate would be to see a flame of energy, a flame that glows with so much color, the color disappears and becomes pure white.

It is difficult to describe the subtle body of someone who is not developed. The particles are floating in a stream of en-

---

[3]The subtle body projects itself to the different plains or worlds during sleep and while meditating.

ergy that is far more dense and neither refined nor luminous. The body itself would seem to be heavier, more dense, and very drab in color. This type of subtle body cannot travel far in the subtle world, so the body itself is usually kept close to the physical one. Such an individual is completely immersed in the mundane and in the lower nature. Because life experience is reflected in the subtle body, it will change its nature, but it will take many hundreds of lifetimes for that to happen.

Evolution is a slow process in the eyes of humankind, and a much faster process when one understands the universe. The universe itself is billions and billions of years old, and one series of life patterns is very small in comparison. Also, when we talk of the evolution of the spirit, we refer to the spirit incarnating on this planet only. Every planet has its own evolutionary pattern to be fulfilled, and therefore, each planet is different according to its position in the universe.

As the soul evolves spiritually, it reflects within itself every experience it has had—both positive and negative. The soul has a need for balance and synthesis, so that one series of patterns is not stronger than another. By balancing all the patterns, an individual soul becomes one with the infinite. The striving of the soul toward this oneness becomes stronger as the subtle body becomes more refined. Again, there is a reciprocal set of patterns reflecting on each other. As the individual develops, this reflection changes the dharmic and emotional psychological patterns of the incarnating soul.

To explain this concept more fully it would be best to think of a tree with many branches. The branches are intertwined, and as the tree grows in the sun, the leaves coming forth become fuller and more dense and almost indiscernible in their thickness. So, too, the developed soul with its many, many patterns has a greater capacity to blend itself with the other patterns within it. The more experience we have within, the easier it becomes for us to do our vocations and to understand our emotional natures. Each as it grows becomes more refined, more developed and more synthesized with the other.

The result of fulfilling one's vocation reacts on the spirit and on the psychological patterns, as well. All three certainly reflect an interaction within the individual at all times. This interaction will result in both physical and subtle body changes. If someone has harmony within, then the physical body will be functioning in an aligned manner and there will be very little illness. The same is true of the subtle body. The more harmoniously one lives one's life, the more synthesized are the patterns within the subtle body, enabling it to grow and change.

How to Begin to Develop the Subtle Body

Even though you have a subtle body, it doesn't mean you're using it fully. You may not know you can do just that — USE IT. Belief in the subtle body is just the beginning. Next, you must consciously start to work to open it up to the consciousness. This requires a lot of concentration and using that concentration in a very directed way. To begin, do the following exercise:

> *Close your eyes and imagine the subtle body. Do this by first seeing yourself as you appear physically, then letting that image fade into a luminous ball of light.*

Next, take this ball and place it in your heart and say to your higher Self:

> *Please let me experience what my subtle body looks and feels like. What does it contain in the way of energy?*

Then imagine yourself blending, becoming one with the higher Self as you again ask:

> *Please let me experience my subtle body.*

To experience the energy requires more than concentration—
it requires that you become your higher Self, if only for a
moment. Practice this until you see or feel something, no
matter what it is. Then place this image or feeling in your
heart, ask to be one with it, and try to sense its essence. Remember, in order to do this you must be completely quiet,
with little emotion. Naturally, if you are irritated at all, you
will not be able to make the connection with your higher Self.

Try this and don't be discouraged if you have trouble seeing the subtle body at first. If you have not been using it, it
may take time to awaken to your consciousness. Do not be
disturbed by its shape or if it changes. Changes are due to its
molecular nature; the subtle body is not anything you may
think it to be.

When you work with the subtle body, it may suddenly
change its form completely. Let it happen and just watch,
making no inward judgments.

Enjoy the experience and simply realize you are many
things at different times and that these things will reflect
themselves in your subtle body. You will know it is within you
when you feel a vibration through the physical body. Do not
be fearful when that happens. Just relax and fully experience
the energy.

6

INTEGRATING THE THREE ASPECTS

Each aspect or pattern that has been mentioned — specifically, work, psychological and spiritual patterns — will be helped when understood and worked with separately, but there must come a time when all three should be looked at as a group that needs to be integrated. To do this requires that you consciously strive toward a complete synthesis with the higher Self.

Naturally, this is a long process. As the soul develops, it requires more and more energy to change itself, and this energy comes from the higher Self. Therefore, it is always important to link with the higher Self when consciously delving within. A positive exercise would be as follows:

> *Link with the higher Self.*[1] *Get a clear picture of your vocation. Again experience yourself working at it. Be aware of all the steps you need to take in order to accomplish it. Now imagine yourself successfully accomplishing your life's work. What is that like for you? How does it make you feel?*

Are you feeling happy, for example, or is there something interfering with your sense of happiness or accomplishment? If that is the case, stop the process and ask your higher Self:

---

[1]See the higher Self exercises, chapter 1, pp. 4-7.

Show me what it is that is blocking my having positive feelings. What is interfering? Then ask your higher Self, *Is there anything else I need to know at this time?*

Another exercise would be as follows:

Link with your higher Self. Again imagine yourself doing your life's work and try to sense, at the same time, your subtle body accompanying you in your work. Try to sense its presence working with you. How is this different from the first exercise?

When you have successfully done the first two exercises, do the following exercise:

Link with your higher Self. Imagine yourself doing your vocation. Now feel fully what it's like to do the work, and at the same time feel your subtle body with you, helping you. Again, is there a difference?

In a similar manner, if you are actually doing your life's work, stop for a moment and connect with the psychological patterns in you. Try to feel what they are like and then connect with the subtle body, allowing it to be with you so that you are consciously using all three. This type of visualization helps in integrating the three sets of patterns within your makeup.

You will sense if any of the patterns are blocked when you do this exercise. Before resuming your work, it's important to work through any block because it will interfere with your sense of accomplishment, which is very important for personal development.

Observe your feelings and deeper emotions while involved in this process. It is these deeper emotions that can block success. Look at yourself from a detached viewpoint, allowing for the luxury of simply "being," pausing in those moments to observe and absorb everything you see and feel.

Never be in a hurry to synthesize these parts. Invariably, if you wish to finish quickly it will not be accomplished. Use your intuition to help you understand what is needed next. Let it be a guide while working with the three aspects.

It's difficult to understand the complexity of a human's makeup. It is far more intricate than what is known to science. The physical makeup is never complete unless it's possible to see alongside it the subtle body with its special composition. The complexity of the subtle body relates to how evolved the individual is. Therefore, this complexity can contain several blocks to awareness. The more evolved a person is, the harder it is to see some of the blocks, only because they may have happened many thousands of years ago. As a person develops, the blocks need to surface and be removed, if the subtle body is to continue its spiritual growth.

If for some reason you are still blocked when you work with the exercises in this chapter, and you ask to remove the blocks or know what they are, and you still only see blocks, then that is an indicator that you need to work differently. Simply connect with your higher Self and ask it to show you a different way in which to work to integrate the three patterns within you.

7

Letting Your Work Happen

When you have discovered your vocation and have gone through the different processes outlined in the previous chapters, then you can clearly pursue the work. There may still be problems and obstructions, however, particularly if the work in any way interferes with the daily routine. For example, if you discover your work is to become a sculptor and you have a full-time job and a family to support, how can you proceed, given that these responsibilities must be the first consideration?

There is a series of patterns within the soul that is set into motion at birth. These patterns contain many bits of information that form a life. The age when an individual is to begin his or her vocation would be one of these bits. If a person uses free will[1] to change the pattern, the bits rearrange and form a new series of patterns to accommodate the change. The sculptor may have been destined to develop his or her vocation and be married later in life. Instead, using free will he or she chose to marry young and have a family. Because he or she cannot afford to do this work while providing for a family, the timing has changed. The sculptor may have to wait

---

[1]Free will is the ability of the individual to manifest his own destiny. This can often be in opposition to the pre-ordained destiny established before birth. The use of free will can sometimes change that destiny or affect its timing. When used positively, it can affect karma.

a few years, until his or her family is grown, before pursuing this vocation. In the meantime, if this need to sculpt is strong enough, he or she will accelerate training by sending the subtle body to study on the subtle plane.[2]

Age doesn't matter when it comes to vocation. Even if a person begins the work much later in life, the feeling of achievement will be the same. Remember, this doesn't mean success in the eyes of the world, but rather success felt in the consciousness of the individual. Therefore, a person may have done only two or three years of the vocation before leaving the earthly body, but if those two or three years fulfilled the inner need, the individual will die feeling a sense of achievement in terms of the life's work.

I cannot emphasize too much the importance of the life's vocation, even if it's discovered only later in life. It makes a great difference in the spiritual growth of the individual. The following case illustrates this point.

> One of my most enthusiastic clients was a woman in her mid-50s. Ann had raised a family and now felt bored. She wanted to jump into something new and exciting. When she meditated on what her vocation could be, what came up were a few symbols — one was a rose, the other a sickle.

> Placing the rose in her heart, she had a vision in which she saw herself sitting in a bedroom in her present home, but the bedroom was an office. Ann was writing at a computer, stopping now and then to look out the window at her rose garden. When I asked her to try to see what she was writing, she felt blocked and could see nothing at all.

---

[2]The subtle body is capable of accumulating knowledge in the subtle world and impressing that knowledge into the consciousness of the individual.

I next had her place the sickle in her heart. The sickle was a bit more difficult to unravel; she could see only vague images, but she kept at it with high spirits. Finally, Ann saw a peasant's outfit which made her think she might be picking up a past life, but the next image was that of a modern library.

I then took her through a process in which I suggested that she envision the library, walk inside and slowly look at the books on the shelves. Ann saw the books clearly and, picking one up off the shelf, saw to her surprise that it was written in Russian. I asked her to examine it more closely and when she did she saw her name on it. It was quite a shock! Ann had always been good at languages, had even studied Russian when she was younger, but never in her wildest dreams had she ever thought about developing that ability.

With further process work, Ann discovered her vocation was to be a translator, and she happily went back to college to further her abilities. Ann's need to go on and do her work was so strong it carried her through many blocks that related to rearranging her personal life so as to do the new work.

To do your vocation in a focused and constructive manner requires that you give yourself totally to the work. There is no such thing as over-doing. If you are truly working at something that is part of your inner destiny, then hard work will not affect you in any way. Hard work can only enervate you when you are working in a job that isn't right for you. To understand this, look at how you feel when you're doing a specific job you know is wrong for you. Nothing seems right, and a lot can go wrong. But it all falls into place when it is part of your inner striving.

In fact, rarely do you have problems with doing your life's work, but don't mistake accomplishment elsewhere with doing the vocation. You may achieve a very high status in a particular job and do very well at it, and still not be doing your vocation. The feeling of doing well will give you a sense of self, but no matter how important the job is, if it is not the life's work you will always feel something is wrong with it.

There is also a tendency to think that worldly success means happiness. How untrue this is! Life itself is only the means for bringing forth an inner sense of "be-ness" or Self, the experience of wholeness and inner peace that comes when one is fulfilling one's full potential.

And don't think the reality of life is always clearly defined. In the nuances you can often discover the correct manner of living. The achievement of success frequently brings difficulties, yet if you have a vocation that is meant to include worldly success, there will not be a problem in achieving it. You will feel difficulty despite such success only when you are destined to do other work and have not done it.

Nearly everyone on the planet has lived in many different types of circumstances, which include a range from very wealthy to very poor. Often, money is sought because it represents a way of life that brings pleasure. But true, inner pleasure can only come from the spirit, and that may require a simple life in which there is little in the way of worldly goods. If great wealth is achieved with no feeling of attachment to it, then there will be a greater chance to find inner happiness. Much depends on the spiritual essence. Seeking to do well and have certain pleasures as a consequence is fine. Here, money is simply a way to achieve, not the means or the end result.

If an individual relinquishes his or her vocation to have money, then he or she will truly be unhappy at a later time in life. Never will worldly goods replace the feeling of accomplishing the chosen vocation, and never will the vocation be relinquished without deep feelings of regret. And those feelings of regret will stay with the soul after it dies and come in again with the individual in the next life, causing feelings of unworthiness and inferiority. Therefore, doing one's vocation no matter what the circumstances is very important.

It is never necessary to force this, simply plan to do it at a later time if the time now is not right. Don't sacrifice everything for your vocation; it won't be satisfactory. If you give up home and family and all the things you love to pursue work that will not allow you to be with them, then you will feel great unhappiness in doing the work. It is much better to wait until the right time. What's important is to clearly know in your heart that the work will some day be done.

And don't pursue your life's work without thinking how it will affect others. Always be aware of karmic involvements that can certainly be affected by the work. If you inadvertently hurt someone or cause someone to be thrown out of a position he or she needs and deserves to have, you will have incurred negative karma. It is always better to wait until the right time, to disturb the least number of people by your pursuit.

How many have "succeeded" in doing their work but have stepped on others to do so? As a result, the inner spirit feels a sadness for having hurt others, and though the vocation has been fulfilled, the soul will die with a sense of sadness, which will affect the incarnating individual.

Always, the work must be done at a time when it can best be achieved with the least opposition, opposition that is often caused by vibrations coming from the planet. If this is the case, then no matter how hard you try to do your work, things will always go wrong. For example, if you are meant to discover a cure for a certain disease, the cure will not be discovered until the cure is meant to happen. Therefore, no matter how many scientists work on finding a cure for this disease, it simply will not be found until the planet's karma accepts it, karma that relates to the planet's own evolutionary patterns.

The work still has to go on, but someone who is in tune with the planet will have a sense of when the time is right to pursue it. This sense comes from an inner balance with the forces of nature. Always stay in touch with those forces and the vocation will take place naturally, at the proper time and the proper pace.

It is true that there is nothing completely new on Earth. Everything changes but has a base that goes on through eternity. It is this basic essence that gives a sense of awareness of when the time is right. Let your intuition indicate when the time is here. Have the patience to understand that everything has its place and the place cannot change simply because you want it to. To push and force the work to be done can only cause feelings of frustration. Always accept life as it presents itself. Never expect nature and the forces of nature to change the patterns of evolution. Only hope you can unite your energies with those forces and come to a deeper realization of how you can best work with them in cooperation and unity. Then your life will flow in a stream of contentment.

The laws of nature will always affect your work because you are part of nature—not separate. You are part of the forces on the planet. Your subtle body works with those forces and relates them back in a manner that affects everything you do. Allow yourself the perception needed to understand this. Let your subtle body be part of your consciousness, and you will never deviate from the flow of life.

8

Overcoming Personal Obstacles

It is not uncommon to discover what the true vocation is and then feel unworthy of it. For example, if you are supposed to be a spiritual teacher, so very often the role is not achieved because of feelings of unworthiness. This is also true in regard to a professional life. The knowledge of what it requires to become a lawyer, doctor, business manager, or any professional who requires higher learning can impede your striving to accomplish this vocation. Moreover, many professions require extensive schooling and for some this schooling, in itself, brings up resistance and fear.

This is particularly true for those who have found out about their vocations after having already gone through school and who have had jobs for several years. How very difficult it is for them to honestly commit themselves to leaving their jobs and returning for additional schooling! Particularly if they are over the age of 30, it requires a great deal of inner striving to do such a thing.

How can this be helped, how can such people be made to believe in themselves enough to return to college or to go on for a higher degree than has already been obtained? Too often they will simply say it is impossible, that there is no way they can re-enter the classroom and feel comfortable with younger students. They've been finished with school for years, and it's just not worth it.

This attitude is very common, particularly with men. A woman who has raised a family will often feel the need to begin a new career, but even for such a woman it will require a lot of inner courage to venture forth. A man is much more apt to feel it's impossible and will stay in a job he dislikes until he feels so unhappy and is in such a crisis that he is forced to re-examine his life simply to go on. These crises have been written about in psychology books and are often described as the mid-life crisis, or the existential crisis, in which an individual is totally unhappy with everything he or she is doing. The following example illustrates this.

Mason had always hated being an accountant. He really wanted to be a school teacher and only became an accountant because his father insisted that he follow in his footsteps. The father's influence was so strong he didn't have the courage to oppose him.

When Mason reached 45, he decided he'd had enough; he was going to make a lot of money, get out and enjoy the rest of his life the way he wanted to. At that time everything was going beautifully for him. He managed and owned his own accounting company, which was doing very well. He had a good reputation in the field, was liked and highly respected by his workers and clients.

Mason had absolutely no understanding of the stock market or investments. He had never invested anything at all, but when someone gave him a tip about a new company in town that had a lot of promise, without seeking any advice he took massive loans on his business and literally invested all the money he had in this company.

He never mentioned the investment to his family — a wife and two children — as he wanted to surprise them with his "killing." He told me about it with excitement and in the naive belief that everything would work out well. I questioned his actions and tried to warn him, but he just couldn't hear me. It was like listening to a man being evicted, with the furniture being hauled out beside him, talking about a lavish party he was giving at his home on the weekend.

Well, it was a surprise all right! The company failed and Mason lost everything, including his business, which went to creditors. The house was in his wife's name, so he was able to keep that, but it had to be mortgaged to meet bills. In a matter of one year, Mason went from being a very wealthy, successful businessman to having nothing.

Here's a case of someone so pressured by work he hated that he lost clear thinking. Mason was really having a nervous breakdown, which followed in full force when everything was gone. Unfortunately, he never fully recovered to the point where he could pursue the career he had always wanted—simply to be a school teacher.

Such crises are often related to the soul's need to express itself, in order to do the work it is meant to do. The discontentment felt in mid-life can be just that, the soul nudging a person to stop doing the present work, to look within and find out what the real vocation is. This can cause a real transformation if the person delves sincerely into the deeper self. But if the individual simply feels unhappy and discontented without self-examination, then a mental breakdown can happen, or a debilitating illness, which can be a way of escaping. Facing inner knowing can be so frightening, in fact, that some individuals will do anything to avoid it.

If going through a crisis results in a deeper awareness of self, then we become much stronger with healthier feelings. It is at this point that we can find the courage needed to undertake additional education. Usually, people in this circumstance really do well and excel. There is seldom a desire to shirk studying or to work in a half-hearted way. It is, indeed, wonderful to see older people develop at a time when their life is almost over. When these individuals really connect with the vocation, everything will be done to fulfill it in the remaining years. The crisis that was experienced only helps to strengthen the will. Nothing can ever be as difficult again.

If you feel your vocation is much too demanding, just look at others who have achieved far more at an older age. You never have a vocation you are not capable of doing. You may start working on it when very young, or you may be retired from the work field and begin on it at that time. Fulfilling it is based on when it is best for you to begin and when you can best achieve it. For example, if the earthly time is not ready for an invention, then the inventor will not be able to bring it in. This inventor may have lived a very simple life and, suddenly, in his or her 60s or 80s, invent something that affects the whole planet. The vocation was to discover the invention when the planet was ready to receive it.

Some vocations are very much connected with the evolution of the planet. As I said before, no matter how frequently someone tries to do something, if it is not in keeping with the evolutionary patterns of the planet it cannot be done. The same is true in all fields—the arts, sciences, philosophies. Every one of these is connected to the planet's evolution. New forms and new ways of doing things constantly change, according to changing patterns. The right combination of matter to form something new can only take place when the vibration of the planet is in tune with it.

There is always an unseen force of energy connected to anything new being discovered or being invented. This energy has been formed over the thousands of billions of years the planet has existed. Only when the energy has achieved a certain level can it evoke and combine with other elements to form new possibilities. The new elements will slowly be brought into being as they are attracted from outer space to the planet, which in return is sending out similar vibrations.

The planet evolves slowly, as does the species, but each period of time is relative to the universe and also to the evolution of the Sun and the planets in our galaxy. Time in the universe is measured very differently from time on Earth. What to a human is billions of light-years is simply a flash by the universe's measurement.

The individual whose vocation is to work with the energy of the planet in such a manner will generally be sensitive to what is happening all around and will know when it is right to do something, rather than just think about it. That individual will be much closer to nature and the elementals.[1] Such an individual, from childhood, will have the ability to see elementals, or nature spirits and has been given these abilities to help the self later on. The vocation here is related to the planet itself, because of this wonderful sensitive attraction. These are the geniuses that make great discoveries. Pythagoras, Paracelsus, Galileo, Newton, and Einstein are some. And certainly there are many, many others going back into antiquity. These individuals are very special because their work affects so many.

When man and woman began their cycle of life on this planet they were more ethereal in form. They were also closely connected to nature and the elementals, being made up of similar properties. As they evolved on the planet, their bodies became more densified, which caused the separation of the subtle body from the physical body. When this happened, the physical essence prevailed and the mind, which also had de-

---

[1]The elementals or "Spirits of the Elements" are discussed in *Theosophical Glossary* by H.P. Blavatsky: "The creatures evolved in the four kingdoms or Elements—earth, air, fire, water. They are called by the Kabbalists: Gnomes (of the earth), Sylphs (of the air), Salamanders (of the fire), and Undines (of the water). Except for a few of the higher kinds, and their rulers, they are rather forces of nature than ethereal men and women" (Los Angeles, CA: The Theosophy Co., 1973, p. 111).

veloped, lost its ability to hold on to the more subtle realities. Thus the separation from nature took place. The heart chakra never became attached to the physical, so it was able to maintain its link to the higher worlds and the nature kingdoms. Therefore, it is through the channel of the heart that one can connect back to nature.

If everyone were to begin to work with nature, life would be much easier. There is a way of doing things with an awareness of the elements that helps the work. Too many people force themselves to do things that are totally against their inner natures and don't flow with the energy.

You can best pursue your vocation when it feels right and when you know, in your heart, that you are working without obstruction. We have just discussed the obstruction caused by trying to work when the planet isn't ready for the work. Other, psychological, blocks discussed earlier may also have to be transformed. If after doing the visualizations and getting through obstructions you find that it's still difficult to begin, it simply may be that the time is wrong. Link with the higher Self[2] and ask:

> *It's clear to me what my vocation in life is. Can you please indicate when I am to start working on it?*

The higher Self, which is very much a part of nature, will bring that knowledge to you and tell you when to begin. If the indication is now, then you will have to go back and work more on your obstructions so you can clear the way.

This is all part of destiny. As I explained before, the timing of your life's patterns is planned. The freedom to change the timing is always there, but, inevitably if you go off in one area you will be pulled back — like a rubber band that is stretched and comes rebounding back into place once it's let go. Rubber bands are very changeable, very expandable, and can go in any direction; but they will always bounce back

---

[2]See the higher Self exercises, chapter 1, pp. 4-7.

when released. The same is true when you follow your destiny. Your free will may take you off in many directions, but somehow you will return at another point and continue going in the right manner as the following example illustrates.

Ellen is close to 60. She has spent most of her life working as a psychologist and enjoys her work very much. She has a master's degree but always wanted to get a doctorate in psychology. This urge was there for many years, but for some reason or other she felt blocked in going for it. Finally, in her mid-50s, Ellen enrolled in an external degree doctorate program.

During the first year, on one of her visits to the university, she was sitting on the lawn when a new acquaintance walked by, grabbed her hand and said, "You must come to this lecture with me. The professor is wonderful and he's introducing a new program on systems theory." Ellen went and, as a result, changed her doctorate from psychology to systems, which in turn resulted in a complete career change.

In her younger years, Ellen had been a 1960s hippie. She had gone the whole route, giving up everything to move to the country and live in nature. But, she hadn't been able to support herself and family with just making T-shirts, which is why she gravitated to becoming a therapist. And though the area in which she lived had quite a few corporations, never in her poorest times had she considered getting a job in one. She avidly disliked the corporate world.

When she changed her major to (human) systems theory, Ellen decided to combine it with her background in psychology and work in communities. She started her doctoral thesis, which was also on community, but just couldn't get it off the ground.

In the meantime, she found herself working more and more in non-profit organizations. When it was suggested that her work needed to be in corporations, she responded so negatively that she became aware of some strong fears concerning the world of business. In fact, it brought up her own issues of power, which she then had to look at and overcome.

Ellen is now working in a new career as a management consultant initiating new directions in corporations. The combination of psychology and human systems was the perfect mix for this kind of work, which couldn't even have existed twenty years ago. Ellen knows now that her vocation was to do this work, and that everything she had done before was just preparation for it.

Your life's plan relates to everything that happens to you in childhood, adulthood, and old age. Within that plan are people you are meant to meet, as well as the work you are meant to do. Both may change because of free will, but the main pattern is usually returned to. In fact, there are few who don't follow their destinies in some way or another.

9

THE KARMIC CONTEXT OF YOUR WORK

Most people think that finally understanding their life's work is going to solve all their problems. Knowing our work is certainly the way to personal satisfaction and happiness, but there remains a lot of important work to be done if the vocation is to be fulfilled. So often people discover their vocations and feel wonderful about them, and then fail to do them. The psychological part, mentioned in previous chapters, plays an important part in determining whether a vocation can be fulfilled. Even when this is clear, there are no blocks or problems, and the attitude is right, people may still not be able to do their vocations.

There is yet another factor that always affects the way in which the life's work is fulfilled. This factor is called karma. Karma, which plays a major role in life, is often thought of as involving only cause and effect — we will receive the results of the actions we manifest, positively or negatively, in the present life or a future life. In fact, however, karma is really more than this, because it affects everything we do. This is illustrated in the following case study.

From childhood, Lillian knew her vocation was to be a surgeon. There was never any doubt in her mind. Throughout school she worked conscientiously and made good grades; she had no problem

being accepted by a medical school, and she gradu-
ated with honors.

Lillian then started her internship at a well-known
hospital that was her first choice. From the beginning, her supervisor treated her badly. He obviously
disliked her. He watched everything she did and
found fault with it. She knew it wasn't his general
disposition, because he treated the other interns differently and no one else seemed to be having problems with him. She also knew it wasn't because she
was female, as there were other women in the program who were treated well. Lillian tried talking to
him about what was happening between them but
he only became more nasty. How dare she even
question him?

Fortunately, Lillian was aware of karma, and recognized that this must be an old negative connection.
If she hadn't had this awareness, it could have destroyed her career. She could have become discouraged by his criticism and might have even believed
he was right — that she had no talent to be a surgeon. As a result, she might have switched her spe-
cialization and would not have been doing her real
vocation. Instead, she chose to switch hospitals, in
order to benefit from proper supervision. Lillian is
now a very good surgeon, doing what she always
wanted to do.

If you go into business with someone with whom you have
negative karma, then you have to be very careful that the differences are worked out. Otherwise, they will interfere with
the work.

You need not think of this all the time, otherwise you
will feel uncertain about everything around you. Usually
when there is difficult karma with someone, it will flare up

quickly. At that time you need to re-examine it carefully to determine how difficult it may become. If you literally murdered a person in a past life and the person is now your manager, then you can be fairly sure that person will make your life hell now! It is important in this case to recognize the situation, understand it, learn from it, and quickly leave the relationship. Rarely can this kind of karma be worked through.

There are also some other factors that are karmically influenced. These relate to the personal feelings you have toward yourself. If your karma causes you to avoid power because in a previous lifetime you were powerful and hurt others, then you may feel anxious when it comes to fulfilling your work — particularly if the work will eventually put you in a position of some power.

Realize that power — when used positively — is a force that makes things happen. It is an energy causing change, change that can be positive or negative, constructive or destructive. Many people have lived lives in which they were in positions of authority. Sometimes, people will deal with personal power in a strictly selfish and self-contained manner, using their positions to control others. This is the general consensus of what power represents, specifically, because we have only now evolved to where we can have power and use it constructively to help others and ourselves. Because power means strength of will, it can be frightening. If the strength of will is given to us by our higher Self and the higher Self is the source, then you can be certain this power will be positive. If we let our lower natures, our egos, handle the power, then it will revert back to a destructive force. It's important to realize that when we fear power, it's usually because we have in past lives abused and been abused by it. Often, these types of lives have to be lived and relived to come to a better understanding of the duality of power.

When power is incorporated into your work not only can it enable you to succeed, but also it gives you the impetus to work through the obstacles you will encounter. It is important to look at your past karmic influences and realize how they affect your dealing with power issues. Some people will be so afraid of power that they will unconsciously place themselves in servile positions, whereas others will seek power positions to gratify hidden desires. If this is an issue with you, try an exercise with your higher Self and ask It to reveal to you your feelings about power and where they come from.

In any case, when dealing with karmic influences, it's important to include not only relationships but also personal feelings and psychological needs. This is sometimes difficult when it comes to understanding oneself. If someone has the karma that prevents comprehension, then how can it be overcome? Let's take, for example, an individual who was totally selfish and self-centered in a previous lifetime. The karma in this life will probably be to have relationships with others who are likewise self-centered and who never give that individual any attention or understanding. Often this can cause a personality split. The individual has no understanding of self and has a hard time relating to people. If the vocation is to work with others, the individual will have a hard time succeeding unless the situation is healed. This can happen if the need for self-fulfillment becomes intense. One must then seek help with the problems.

To understand how your karma works with your vocation requires a broadened perception of who you are and who you can become. Certainly, accomplishing the vocation will bring about changes that affect the way you relate to others. If you are born with difficult karma to overcome, but incur good karma in later years, it will change and influence your work. Therefore, besides being aware of the karma you have to play out, it is important to be conscious of the karma you are creating on a daily basis. If you do good deeds, the good karma incurred will most certainly help you to fulfill your vocation. Here is another example of how karma can affect your vocation.

Alex was in his early 20s. He was obviously very insecure, unsure of himself, with absolutely no idea of what he wanted to do in life. Every time we did a visualization, he would see a banner that read "Vote for Alex." When he placed the idea of becoming a politician in his heart, it felt great. Frankly, though, it seemed absurd to both of us. Alex hated college, had dropped out, and definitely disliked anything "establishment." His background was difficult. He had been placed in foster homes for most of his childhood, homes in which he had been abused. His father finally claimed him when he was a teenager, but that also was a very bad relationship. For Alex to overcome those karmic scars seemed much too difficult.

Putting the political career aside, we continued to work with imagery to determine if there was something else in him that hadn't been uncovered, but nothing came up. Maybe he was meant to work in an office for a politician? We worked with that by going through a day's work, but each time he tried to see himself working for a politician, the image changed into himself as the political leader.

I was concerned that Alex was trying to fulfill some ego desires, so we did some special work to be certain this wasn't the case. Every time we put the politician in his heart, the response was positive. We finally realized it had to be right.

Negative karma will affect someone's life's work. In Alex's case, I knew it would require intensive psychological help for him to achieve the self-confidence needed for such a profession. He agreed to undergo therapy and is now developing a healthier self-image. Pursuing his vocation at this point would only be self-defeating. Only when Alex has achieved a solid sense of self will he be able to go back to school and begin working successfully toward his goal.

One last karmic connection that needs to be understood is the relationship of the individual to the work itself. Certainly, if someone has done this work before, the subtle body will contain those patterns of knowledge. Part of achieving success would be to consciously reawaken that knowledge and use it again. It will positively be of great help in carrying out the work successfully. It is also important to know if the work has not been done before — if it is something totally new. If so, the person will have to work harder. It doesn't mean the individual cannot achieve success, it just might take a little longer. Again, it is attitude that matters. If the person who has the inner knowledge and experience refuses to work at uncovering and bringing it up from within, then that person is put in a similar position to not having had the learning experience. It is always important to use the accumulations from the past.

If you haven't seen a past life that is similar to your vocation, link with your higher Self[1] and ask:

My vocation in this life is _____. Please show me if at any time in the past I have done this work.

If you hear or see a verification, then ask your higher Self:

Please tell me how I can best reawaken this knowledge from the past.

Continue to ask with each answer until you have a definite way that will help you begin to utilize your previous knowledge. The method is always specific to the individual which is why it's best to be told by your higher Self.

---

[1]See the higher Self exercises, chapter 1, pp. 4-7.

10

Seeing into Karmic Influences

The previous chapter discusses the importance of realizing that karma can interfere with or help your life's work. To understand this, imagine a ship floating on water, moving with the current, not against it. This ship can be equated to the vocation. The water is the life's energy needed to help fulfill the vocation, and the current in the water is the karmic pattern. If your karma is good and you know your vocation, the energy will be there for you to do it. But if you have negative karma to be encountered along the way, then the currents will turn backward and literally stop the flow of energy, causing you to confront blocks in the work you are meant to do.

Instead of thinking of karma as being something separate that you must always deal with, try thinking of it as currents and threads which are part of everything you do. These currents will flow, making things easy, or they will be destructive, causing conditions to be difficult. To become sensitive to the currents within you, try to become consciously aware of them. If you have some very good relationships with people you love, recognize the beneficial exchange of energy between you as positive karma. Also be aware of the antithesis. When you meet someone to whom you feel an inner resistance, this can indicate there is negative karma between you. Completely feeling what this means only happens when you consciously recognize it and begin to work to change it. The following story illustrates only one example of how this energy can work in your life.

Amy was on a three-week tour of Europe. She was traveling alone but wanted to save some money, so she signed up for a double room to share with another single woman, Maryjean. It took only one day for her to realize that Maryjean was extremely difficult and was acting antagonistically toward her for no apparent reason. When she watched her with other people, Amy saw that Maryjean behaved in a friendly and nice manner.

Amy tried to switch rooms and was willing to pay extra for a single, but the accommodations were all booked. She was stuck with Maryjean. Being as nice as she could, Amy confronted Maryjean and asked her if there was something wrong that was causing her unpleasant behavior toward Amy. It was impossible! Maryjean just made excuses and continued to be bitchy.

By this time Amy was aware that this was a negative past relationship. How frustrating to be stuck in a situation that could easily ruin her vacation! Amy was determined not to let it happen. Every time Maryjean was negative toward her, she made a careful effort to respond in a very positive, light-handed manner, deliberately not allowing herself to take it personally.

Maryjean was not at all conscious of what was happening, but because Amy went out of her way to be friendly and nice, she slowly softened her attitude toward her. They obviously would not be bosom friends, but they did manage to go through the rest of the vacation with greater harmony.

Becoming sensitive to your life's energy is the way to proceed. Literally, this means that the psychic energy[1] emitted from your physical body, coming from a part connected to your subtle body, is allowed to flow freely if there are no physical or psychological blocks. Both the physical and the subtle body are very much affected by karmic patterns that attract or repel throughout life. If there is no understanding of these patterns, then circumstances will always seem to happen to you. They will be a surprise that can't be controlled. But, if there is conscious recognition of the patterns within, your intuition will perceive when something is going to happen, allowing you time to prepare to face the experience. The psychological as well as the physical are interconnected and are totally affected by the flow of psychic energy from within.

Often someone will work to make his or her body physically fit and will still come down with an illness when it is least expected. This is because the person is not recognizing the emotional blocks that are operating against the physical. Sometimes physical ailments are caused by inner fears and insecurities. Unless those fears are understood and allowed to be aired, they will certainly affect the body.

In order to come closer to synthesizing all three — the physical, psychological and spiritual — it is necessary to develop an awareness of how your energy is flowing. Try doing the following exercise:

> *Imagine or visualize yourself standing naked in front of you.*

---

[1]In *Letters of Helena Roerich,* psychic energy is discussed as follows: "You know that psychic energy is called PRIMARY energy, therefore it includes all other energies, which are only its differentiations.

"Thus, Parafohat is the fundamental, or primary psychic energy in its highest cosmic aspect, and Fohat is its next aspect in the manifested Universe. The same psychic energy manifested as life force is diffused everywhere as PRANA" (New York: Agni Yoga Society, 1967, vol. 2, p. 331).

Then connect with your heart chakra and ask your higher Self:[2]

Please look at my physical body and show me or let me experience if and where there are any obstructions.

Practice this, then take a piece of paper and draw an outline sketch of your body. If you see or sense that there is a block somewhere in your body, then consciously focus all your attention on the spot and look at it. You can draw it on the paper in color. Try to sense what it means. Ask your higher Self:

Is this block in _____ color psychological or has it manifested into the physical?

After getting an answer, ask:

Can you tell me more about it?

Keep questioning until you develop a deeper understanding of its cause. This is very good to practice throughout your life on a regular basis. It can often help avoid illness and help discover any blocked emotions.

Psychic energy literally brings all the parts of the body into perfect working order. It reflects back to the subtle body and impresses on that body what is occurring in the physical one. Therefore, if you have an illness in the physical body, it will in turn rearrange the patterns of the subtle body to reflect the illness. This is why, for instance, when someone's arm is amputated, the pain of the arm will remain in the subtle body and reflect itself back to the physical, so the person will still feel physical pain in the area where the arm used to be. This has never been medically explained because most doctors

---

[2]You may use one of the higher Self exercises, chapter 1, pp. 4-7, to first connect with the higher Self. When you have made the connection, then visualize your naked body standing in front of you both. You can also try just connecting to the heart chakra and sending the question up to the higher Self.

have never understood that to cure the physical field you also have to cure the subtle body, through the use of psychic energy. The subject of healing with psychic energy is only recently being understood, and still needs to be accepted by the medical profession.

The subtle body has within its makeup the ability to work with and affect the physical body which in turn impacts it. Awareness of the subtle body heightens the perception of what is happening in the physical. Connecting the heart to the higher Self literally means connecting with the spiritual Self, contained in the subtle body, and allowing it to be absorbed fully within. Consciously working with the higher Self helps you live your daily life and aids spiritual growth.

11

Understanding Karma and Your Vocation

How karmic patterns relate to the vocation and how important it is to be aware of them is described in previous chapters. The best way to understand karma is to think of it as a very definite action requiring a response. Any action done in past lifetimes has attracted a definite response, whether it be good or bad. How your past lives were lived will define the accumulation of negative or positive karma you carry over into this life.

Usually, most people who have evolved to the point at which they are working with their subtle bodies have a balance of both negative and positive karma. This means they have gone through lifetime after lifetime experiencing both and are now born with a balance.

In fact, sometimes an individual has accumulated positive karma to the extent that the life is extremely easy. The individual is born into good psychological conditions and a loving family, so the childhood is full of good conditioning. This person will undoubtedly find it easy to do the life's work and will encounter few obstacles.

Someone who has a balance of both the positive and negative karmic patterns will experience a little more difficulty but can also, once the vocation is known, break through the difficulties and achieve it.

How vocation and karma work together can be likened to a wind-up toy. A particular toy's mechanism or gears that cause the action to happen can be likened to the karmic imprint on the physical organism. When the wind-up coil (which is similar to the psychic energy) is in contact with the mechanism, this causes the action of the toy. The action is likened to life's work. This kind of interaction in the toy works well until the toy breaks down. Likewise with a human being, the inner action can also work very well until something happens psychologically to stop the action, such as the loss of a loved one, a physical illness, or a natural catastrophe.

There is also the responsibility the individual has toward his or her family and country. If a person's country goes to war, he or she may have to fight, and can be either hurt or killed as a result. All of these things are karma — part of the individual's patterns — but sometimes the karma happens as a result of right circumstances.

For example: A particular individual may be meant to die in a war because in a previous life he loved war and killing. His karmic patterns contain the information that he is to be killed in a war at a later time. This person may be destined to do a certain vocation at a particular time, but if unforseen circumstances cause his country to go to war — circumstances resulting from the country's karma — the person will die at this time because his karma contains it. If there could have been, instead, an avoidance of war, which is also possible, then he would have been able to fulfill his vocation and die normally. He would still, however, have to be killed in a war in a future lifetime.

The karma of a country is similar to that of an individual. Every action produces a response. The results of what it has done will often cause its destruction. During a country's growth, the karma is usually positive. In time there may occur a balance of karma, negative and positive, or it can become unbalanced. If the karma is more negative, a country might find itself with enemies making war against it.

The karma of the country in which you are born relates to you directly. In order to fulfill your vocation, the conditions in which you live — also the country — must help make it possible. We can illustrate this in the following example.

A person living in a country where there is very little opportunity for creative freedom will find it difficult to fulfill the vocation of being a writer. The karma may have placed the person in this type of country because it was necessary to go through difficulty, or perhaps the experience of former lifetimes there attracted the person back at a time when the country was still free. A child born in Hungary at the time of the Second World War, was born in an independent country. The result of the war put the country in the hands of the Russian state, which changed Hungary's political structure. So the individual who was meant to be a writer and have the freedom to express ideas when growing up would be in a difficult position in Hungary after the Second World War.

This is just an example of how national karma can change a person's whole life structure. The individual who was meant to be a creative writer will come back again in a different place and fulfill the vocation. The person will also be able to pay off some personal negative karma as a result of being prevented from doing the work. No experience in life is lost.

Be aware of the relationship between karma and your life's work. It is wise to always be conscious of the people around you who will affect your work, as well as the community, the city, the state, and the country in which you live. If you feel your country is making negative karma through wrong decisions and actions, it is important to protest, in order not to be tied into the country's karma. Protesting will break the karmic link. Keep in mind the human values, the values connected to your sense of right and wrong.

The balance between your karma and life's work requires surroundings that allow them to work together. Any circumstance, be it a disruptive home or a disruptive political system, will affect your doing the work and finding personal happiness.

Certainly, being in a destructive relationship is the most common way of impeding growth. You may be surrounded by people who are not compatible with you, which also can impede and restrain your work. Often these people are old karmic ties that never have been resolved, but there will also be times when you will be with people who come from completely different cultural backgrounds — backgrounds that have conditioned their way of behaving. You may find yourself born into a family of a certain ethnic background that feels alien to you. This could be because it's your first experience with that culture. All of this is karma, but the way in which you handle it determines how it will affect your work. Differences can be challenging and exciting or they can be annoying.

12

UNSUPPORTIVE RELATIONSHIPS AND YOUR WORK

A previous chapter discussed your karmic relationships with the people around you and their effect on your life's work. The relationships depicted were general ones. This chapter will deal with relationships that are more personal and how they can often be a karmic influence, as well as prevail upon your vocation. A good illustration of relationship and vocation is a story told to me by a spiritual teacher:

> Some time ago, in a kingdom in the East, lived a princess who was destined to be married to the king of a neighboring realm. Her destiny was to work with the king and help him rule the kingdom, because he was not too bright and would not be a good ruler. She was the one who had the ability to rule justly.
>
> And though the king realized her talents, he decided at the last minute to marry her sister instead, a sister whose beauty had captured his heart. The sister, unfortunately, was also stupid and could not be of help in ruling the people. As a result, the kingdom fell into distress and was taken over by another king in war.

If the king had followed his destiny and married the first princess, his kingdom would have prospered under her direction and their children would have been raised by her to be good rulers. This kingdom disappeared and was no more after one hundred years, yet it could have become a great dynasty.

The first princess, having not married the king, instead married into another kingdom where she was kept in a servile position. None of her talents or wisdom was used politically, so her vocation was not carried out, though at a later time, in another lifetime, she did come back as a ruler.

The first king could have solved the situation easily. If his desire for the sister was unrelenting, he could simply have made her his second wife as that was a practice of the time.

This is an example of how a single mistaken relationship changed not only the king's vocation, but also affected the many people in his kingdom. If he had been wiser and listened to his advisers, which he did not, then there would have been a different and far better ending to the story.

Often you can be faced with a very profound decision in your personal life. Certainly, becoming involved in a difficult relationship, or an abusive one, cannot only impair your chances of succeeding, but may also make you psychologically impotent. Karma is a major mover in bringing people together for either good or bad, but you need not be pulled back into a difficult or disastrous relationship if you are aware that it is an old negative connection. Awareness is very important because it helps us make the right decisions and understand those decisions in a deeper way.

A man, for example, who is seeking a political career knows from the start that he needs a wife who is emotionally stable, who will be able to work with people and not be afraid of publicity or appearing in public. This man will therefore look for a wife who is poised, sophisticated, intelligent, and able to cope with the demands of a political life. He will choose carefully and not allow attraction or even love to be his major need.

How simple it would be if we all could think of our partner in life in terms of vocation and the need to support each other in performing our life's work. When we are young, mistakes are often made in choosing partners. These mistakes can impede the work and cause emotional damage. Even if we leave a partner, it is often difficult to find the strength of purpose to go on.

Love and attraction are important for a person's well-being, part of feeling happy and content in life. If we do not have love and happiness, we can be caught in a web of self-pity, which blocks being successful in life. It is also important to choose partners who can best help us fulfill our purposes. The following illustrates this point.

Stephanie worked in the corporate world as a highly successful manager in Human Resources. She was intelligent, full of energy and well-liked by her fellow workers.

When she was 28 she met Richard, fell in love, and married him. Both mentioned they wanted children someday, but neither thought or talked about it until Stephanie's 30th birthday. The marriage had been happy to that point, but then the fights began. Stephanie would gladly have a child but didn't want to give up her job and career. Her vision had always been to be a working mother with a nanny and day care for the children.

Richard was appalled at the idea. He felt strongly that a true mother should be at home with the children, at least until they went to school. How could

she be so uncaring and self-centered? It was un-
thinkable that she should want to leave his children
in someone else's care.

Stephanie loved Richard and didn't want the marriage to break up. Totally worn out by the fights
they'd been having, she conceded. Stephanie gave
birth to a baby girl, quit her job and became the
good mother.

The first year or two she decorated the home, sat in
the park with other mothers and nannies and tried
hard to enjoy her new role. But it didn't work. She
became bored. She found she had very little in common with the other mothers. Recipes, toilet training
and "My Johnny did or said this" was the general
theme, a far cry from *The Wall Street Journal* or
Forbes.

She quickly fell into a state of lassitude. Her glam-
orous, well-dressed look became sloppy and uncaring. Two years later no one would have recognized
her. She had gained 30 pounds, let her hair grow
long and straggly down her back and said very little.
Richard always came home late from the office and
complained about the way the house looked. All the
things they once had in common faded with her
looks. Even their lovemaking became a boring routine.

The marriage split up when their second child was
3. Richard was in love with another woman and
Stephanie didn't even care. What she did care about
was being left alone with two small children, very
little money, and no immediate prospects.

It was difficult for Stephanie to get back in shape,
regain her confidence and find a job, but caring for

the children gave her the incentive. Otherwise, she would have just given up. She had lost six years and had to relearn many things. It was like starting all over again. Stephanie finally landed a clerical job in Human Resources and within four years had worked her way back to her previous position.

It was a long break in her career, almost twelve years. In retrospect, Stephanie realized the issue of children should have been brought up and agreed on before marrying. Knowing Richard's attitude at the time would have made a difference. Stephanie feels she never would have agreed to his way of thinking and, if he hadn't understood her needs, then it would have been better not to have married him. It would have saved her years of unhappiness and hardship.

Life has many aspects that need fulfillment, the three most important of these being work, relationships, and personal growth. If any are unfulfilled, it can cause unhappiness. Personal growth relates to an individual's spiritual and intellectual growth. If, for example, a man and woman get married at a very young age and one of them changes and grows in intelligence and wisdom and the other remains the same, these two people will have nothing in common when they are older. The reason why so many marriages end in divorce is because of a lack of communication.

There is another part of life that needs to be fulfilled that relates to karmic relationships. Karma will bring us in touch with people from the past, as well as people we have never known. Both are important and both will influence us in different ways. The karmic relationships are always the most attracting, be they positive or negative. This type of relationship can be extremely sensitive because there are so many hidden factors within it not known consciously. Also, the influence of the karmic relationship is always greater and can sometimes change the newly formed relationship. For example, a woman might meet two men, both of whom she is attracted to and likes. If one is karmic and is, in fact, a negative karmic relationship, she will be more drawn to him than to the other man, who could be an extremely positive relationship. If she knows about karma and works with her higher Self to understand the feelings concerning these two men, the woman would realize the karmic connection should be avoided, and that she would be much happier with the other man in forming a new relationship. Unfortunately, however, people often choose wrong partners because they aren't aware of this. Awareness can assist spiritual growth by helping us avoid the results of our past negative karma.

13

Finally Accepting Your Vocation

At the beginning of this book I mentioned the need to understand your vocation or life's work because it will help you on your evolutionary path. The next step is the acceptance of the work itself. You can prepare the way by doing a little exercise:

Close your eyes and connect with your higher Self.[1]

Ask your higher Self:

Help me accept my vocation.

Try to feel that acceptance in your heart.

Does it feel right to you?

Place the work in your heart and again feel if it is right.

Keep the feeling for at least 5 minutes.

Then ask your higher Self:

Help me to accept the vocation and also to believe I truly recognize what it is.

Place these thoughts in your heart and experience the reaction. If something doesn't feel right about it, again ask your

---

[1]See the higher Self exercises, chapter 1, pp. 4-7.

higher Self to help you accept it, and feel the response in your heart. If there is still something wrong, drop the question and slowly open your eyes.

This exercise is very important. If you feel you know your vocation and have not accepted it fully, then you need to go back to some of the earlier exercises and do them again. If everything feels right, then end the exercise by asking:

Is there anything else I need to know about the vocation at this time?

Another way to check is to connect with the higher Self. This time, link your heart with the higher Self's heart and ask:

Your heart understands and knows my life's work.
Let me feel what your heart feels in knowing this.

Try seeing a light pass from your heart to your higher Self's heart. The feeling should be the same. If it's different from what you felt before, you know more inner searching is needed.

The higher Self knows your vocation but cannot tell you what it is. It can only give you hints. The search must be with the conscious mind and heart, the reason being that if you were told directly it would not help you accept the vocation, particularly if there are blocks preventing you from doing it. Another exercise is:

Look in a mirror. Try looking deeply into your eyes and see the inner you. Concentrate on the pupils and let yourself go quietly inward.

When you feel you have achieved this, ask the inner Self:

What do I need to know further about my vocation?

You can continue questioning:

Is there a psychological problem concerning my vocation that I need to know?

Is there something from the past I need to know about relating to my vocation?

Question the inner you in this manner. If nothing happens, work again with the visualization of the higher Self. Go back and forth between these two exercises.

Another way to obtain information is to actually draw a scene of yourself doing your vocation. It doesn't matter how crude the drawing is:

1) Draw a scene which has you in it.

2) Close your eyes and see or imagine this scene.

3) What is happening?

4) What are you feeling?

5) Do you like what you are doing, or do you have the feeling that something is missing?

If the latter is true, open your eyes and again take up the pencil and draw whatever comes to mind. Even if it is something totally different, it doesn't matter. When you have finished drawing, again close your eyes:

1) Imagine the scene you drew. Get a clear picture or feeling of it. If you are in the scene, try again to sense how you are feeling.

2) If you are not in the scene, try to intuit what the scene means in terms of your vocation.

3) Keep trying this exercise until you sense the something that could be missing.

4) Remember to bring it back to your heart to test the feeling there.

You can always accept a vocation when it is fully revealed. Sometimes the vocation may involve doing a couple of things. If you find out about only one of them, it will feel right but not complete. This is a clue that there are more facets that need to be uncovered. Remember, each clue is important to follow, as in a treasure hunt. Each discovery gives a lead to the next, and the next, until you find the treasure. Make the search fun and don't get discouraged. Believe in the higher Self's ability to help, and realize that when you find out the entire truth it will be at a time when you can accept it totally.

14

INTERPERSONAL DYNAMICS AND YOUR WORK

Now we will discuss relationships and how they can help or hinder your vocation. It has been mentioned before that karmic relationships will affect your vocation, but the associations within the workplace itself can make a tremendous difference as well. If you are working with someone on a project who is not anyone you have been with before in a previous life, you still need to come to a deeper understanding of the person and of the way in which you interact. The following is an example of how work relationships can hinder a vocation.

> Simon was a fine doctor with an excellent reputation. He had received his medical degree in the USA and then went to England to specialize in homeopathic medicine. His practice expanded quickly, which made him decide to open a holistic clinic and bring in specialists in other holistic areas, like nutrition, massage, chiropractic, etc.
>
> Unfortunately, Simon lacked people skills and knew nothing about running a clinic. The staff he'd hired to manage the day-to-day operations were inefficient, argued with each other, and were, in general, rude to the patients. Other practitioners joined the group, in what was supposed to be a community at-

mosphere. Meetings were held on a regular basis to discuss problems, but they were really a farce. Simon was totally in control and only pretended to listen to suggestions.

There were constant complaints from everyone about the staff. Trying to get an appointment was impossible. They never answered the phones, and if they did, a caller would be kept waiting a long time. The way Simon handled the complaints was to hold a meeting and ask his staff to do better. If a specific worker was pointed out as being difficult, he would become protective of the person and not even look into the matter.

The other practitioners stayed for only short periods of time. If the staff was negligent about Simon's appointments, you can imagine how their patients were handled! Each tried to make Simon understand how badly the office was being run, but he lived in his own belief system where everything was all right. He even thought, maybe they're overworked! His solution was to hire more staff, but the new people soon realized the others weren't working very hard, so why should they?

It never occurred to Simon to fire any of them. He was so detached from and oblivious to what was going on he wouldn't even listen to his patients' complaints until finally, after he'd lost many, he was forced to wake up.

Seeking advice, Simon brought in a couple of psychologists to try to get his staff in order, but because of the infighting, getting them to agree to new procedures was virtually impossible. This forced Simon to let a few people go. It was like starting all over, and it took a couple of years before he could get his practice back up to what it had been before. Therapy then helped Simon see some of the mistakes he had made.

Unfortunately, Simon could not develop the clinic again. Its reputation had gone down too far for any practitioners to consider joining him. He still thinks community is a wonderful way to live and work and idealistically longs for it but doesn't have any understanding of how it has to operate. If Simon had waited much longer to make the changes in his staff, he could have lost his chance to develop his career as a leading doctor in his area. Fortunately it didn't come to that.

The following case didn't turn out as well:

Carl's career was politics. He decided to make it his profession in law school. He was bright, enthusiastic and did all the right things: he groomed his appearance; worked on facial expressions and speech-making; researched and joined the right party in his area; then helped others to be elected who rewarded him with some good assignments.

When it was his turn to run for office, he had all the support he needed to win a seat in the state legislature. Carl was on his way up! It was a difficult and busy profession with long hours and no free time. When he hired what he thought was a good staff, he made the mistake of not supervising them enough.

His closest assistant, who did a lot of contact work for him, was corrupt and taking bribes under the table. Carl knew nothing of this until the assistant got too greedy and asked the wrong person for money. It was leaked to the newspapers, an investigation followed, and though Carl was proven to be innocent, the scandal kept him from being re-elected. It ruined a budding career and affected the fulfillment of his vocation.

These stories relate to the need to develop and utilize discrimination. How many times have we made horrendous mistakes about people because of a lack of discrimination? Discrimination is, in reality, the use of intuition with the subtle body. The subtle body contains all the past experiences of our various lives, and it is these past experiences that tell us when to be careful and when something is all right. Intuition will help open the awareness. We can have good intuition and still lack discrimination because we have not lived many lives and therefore do not have enough experience. If this is the case, we will have to rely more on intuition, in order not to make wrong decisions about people.

Someone who has lived more lives (and has a storehouse of past experiences) can turn inward and use that knowledge to get a good sense of what is happening. This individual may not need to use the intuition as much, and may instead rely more on past experiences. But it would be better to use both and be operating at a higher level of awareness.

When someone is working closely with you, take the time to get to know that person. Use your heart to connect with the heart of the other and just feel what this person has in the heart chalice. If there is karma between you, you will feel it almost right away, but don't let a good karmic connection stop you from assessing whether this person is doing the job, is honest, is able to contribute something of the self, etc. Ask all the questions you would of anyone to whom you are giving responsibility. Even if the person holds a higher position, be aware of whether the job is being done and how that will affect your doing your own work.

At the beginning of any relationship, be it with a colleague or a potential friend, take the time to link your heart with the heart of the other and determine the person's essence. If you feel something is wrong, it is a warning to be careful. Don't sever the relationship, but be attentive when you are with this person.

It's also important to spend time with the people you have to work closely with. Get to know them, how their minds work and what they like to do and not do. So many working relationships are strictly work, and the individuals who spend hours together have no idea what their colleagues do in their spare time. Knowing about your colleagues helps you decide whether they can take on certain responsibilities or be relied on. If you need to allocate work, you have to be certain the person will follow through, whether on the job or in a social setting.

How can you develop your ability to understand others in this manner? Simply by listening with the heart to what is truly being said. When you link your heart to someone else's heart, the person will reveal many things, not only with words but also with body movements and physical gestures, which often disclose personality traits. If someone is going through a difficult time and is very tired, the person may sit slouched over and have a very strained look. This is easy to spot. Would you give that worker a lot to do? Of course not. The same holds true when you listen to people eager to do more challenging jobs. They will be alert and cooperative. If you neglect to give them a chance to grow, they will become unhappy and eventually leave.

The same applies if you are in a subordinate position and are trying to grow and learn. You know your future is limited if your superior never allows you to contribute new ideas or work on projects that require your input. This would impede you moving toward your vocation. In such a case it is important to quickly change jobs to improve conditions. Never stay in a job hoping the situation will change in time. A person's attitude toward you is apparent from the beginning, so be careful to notice this and act accordingly.

15

INTEGRATING WORK AND LIFESTYLE

Some people discover their vocation early in life and pursue it without difficulty. If you uncover your vocation later in life, you may need to first look at your life and environment before beginning new work. If your vocation is complicated, it may have to be thought out and planned for carefully. For instance, if you return to college and learn something new, this can be demanding and frightening, as well. The following type of planning can be helpful:

> 1) Look at your daily routine and write down all the things you feel are essential to your life. If you are married, being at home with your mate and family would be one of those things. List everything that is important for your happiness, even if it seems mundane—like going to the movies.

> 2) Next, look at the list and take off one item. Close your eyes and see that particular thing, and see it being erased from your life. For example, if you watch the football games on Sunday, see yourself doing that and then see yourself getting up and turning the TV set off. Feel if it is all right. Does it make you sad, does it make you upset?

> 3) Go on down the list doing the same with every item until you have eliminated those things you feel

you can do without. At another time you can look
at the list again and see if it still feels all right to
have eliminated certain things. And don't feel you
can't put an item back if you find yourself missing it
too much.

This exercise prepares you to make extra time in your life so
you can begin to pursue your vocation. There is often a need
to continue working at a job, so the elimination exercise is
important. Slowly let go of those things you have eliminated.
Don't cut them out all at once. Take one at a time, eliminate it
and feel how it is for you. Then go on to the next. Allow your
heart to tell you when it feels right to go onward, increasing
the pursuit and eliminating items from the list.

Once you have allocated time to begin your new work,
regardless of whether you need additional schooling, you will
have to go through a period of adjustment. To suddenly stop
doing things you are in the habit of doing and begin something totally new can be frightening, as well as upsetting to
the nervous system. It would be best to begin the new work
slowly. If additional schooling is needed, take just one night
course for the first semester. Don't rush it, even if you realize
there is a lot of hard work ahead if you are to be skilled
enough to do the vocation.

Because your change in vocation may require adjust-
ments in your family routine, particularly if you are married
and have children, you need to have long talks with your family to explain exactly what you are doing and why. Let them
ask questions and challenge you. If a family member doesn't
accept that you are changing careers, listen to the reasoning
and try to understand how that person must be feeling. Does
the loved one feel threatened that, if you change careers, then
maybe your love will change? How does this person relate to
your new vocation? Look at that. If you decide to go into
public life and become, for example, a politician, does your
spouse fit in? Does the spouse need to change, also? If so,
then both of you may have to agree to additional education.

If you pursue your career without thinking of how that career will affect those at home, you may find yourself losing what you value the most. So, gently approach your loved ones and help them understand why you need to do this. If they love you they will certainly accept your need and may even agree to look at what they can do to help you. Never force your needs on them, though, and insist they change with you. You will only alienate them. The following example illustrates this.

Eleanor was married, had two teenagers, and worked as a manager of a small clothing store, a position she had once enjoyed. She was bored with her job. While working with me, she became aware that her vocation was to be a writer, a novelist.

She was thrilled and really anxious to begin. Without discussing it with her family first, she quit her job and announced that she was devoting herself full-time to the pursuit of her new career. Realizing that there would be no income from her to help support the household, she informed her husband and children that they had to make do with less money. She also told them she would be going to school full-time and so she could no longer do a lot of the household chores, including shopping and cooking. She said it was up to them to change their lives accordingly.

You can imagine the response! She had dumped so much on her family it was impossible for them to accept or support her goal. The atmosphere, naturally, was full of bitter resentment, but Eleanor didn't care. After all, she had worked many years for them, and, if they couldn't accept what she was doing, it only showed their ingratitude.

Off to school she went! At this time she was 40 and hadn't been in a college classroom for 18 years.

Also, when she'd selected her courses, it hadn't occurred to her that school might be difficult at first, so she'd enrolled in a full schedule. The mistake became obvious during the first week of classes, but she doggedly carried on, trying to prove to everyone she could do it! Every day and night she studied until she was exhausted and irritable.

By this time, her husband was threatening to leave her and the kids were screaming and fighting and being even more demanding than before. It was a nightmare! Eleanor was so unhappy and miserable that she came back from school one afternoon and decided to give it all up. Her dream was shattered. She swept the pieces into a closet and tried to forget the whole thing. But the urge was still there. It kept nagging and nagging at her until she couldn't resist it any longer. By then she was working again, part time, for a doctor. This time, without telling her family, she enrolled in one writing course. She did her homework, which was mainly writing, on her days off, while the kids were in school.

The next year Eleanor felt ready to add another course to her schedule but had to come out of the closet. Feeling anxious and defensive, she gave her family one of her best short stories and told them what she had been doing. For the first time she shared her dream with them and asked if they, as a family, could try working together to help her pursue it. She needed their loving support. Their reaction, though skeptical at first, was much more positive. They enjoyed her short story and for the first time talked about her new career as a possibility.

Eleanor is still going to have to work at her vocation slowly, with patience. She now realizes she has to

make certain the family is not feeling too pressured—their happiness is what gives her the freedom to continue.

If you find the situation you're in to be impossible, and if you
feel it will be too difficult for all involved if you pursue your
vocation, then you may have to wait until the time is right. If
this happens, keep the vocation in your heart. Don't forget it.
Remind yourself that you will work toward it one day. Be certain to have the time set firmly in mind. And when the day
arrives don't let anybody talk you out of it. No matter what
the circumstances, start to pursue your vocation.

Be aware—there will always be people who will try to
dissuade or discourage you. They will insinuate that you
haven't the talent to do the work or may even tell you outright
there are already many in your chosen field who are competent, with years of experience, and how could you possibly
compete with them? Many have lost their dreams by listening
to such advice from well-intentioned friends.

If people have not achieved their own vocation and are
not content, they will be the first to try to talk you out of
yours. Don't listen. But, if the person is someone you love,
ask your loved one to believe in you and understand your
need to aspire to the new work. Ask for support and speak up
when your loved ones get negative about what you are doing.
Remember, this is *your* vocation. It is yours to fulfill.

Never ask people to help you if, from the start, they re-
ject and condemn you for what you're doing. Pursue your
goal quietly, and don't talk about it, particularly if you live
with people who are unsupportive. When they see you are really doing it, then they will more than likely accept the
change. No matter how negative they are, don't allow it to
discourage you or change your feelings of enthusiasm. If you
find the situation too trying, then maybe having a separate
place to study or do your work would be helpful, a place away
from anyone who may be causing you to doubt yourself.

Try to keep calm and unemotional when dealing with loved ones about pursuing your new vocation. Otherwise, you will fall into an emotional environment that will affect your work and cause disturbances in your daily routine. No one can pursue something new in a disruptive, emotional environment. Don't be the one to cause this to happen. If you are always considerate of the other person's feelings, it will facilitate the changes that need to be made if you are to continue successfully. Love your work and your family. Use your heart when things are difficult and not flowing smoothly. It will help you to keep your environment calm during the changes.

16

Owning Your Vocation with Enthusiasm

Pursuing your vocation always requires hard work and dedication. Often it is not clear what you need to do next. One problem may be that the work may require a lot of special schooling, instruction or training, and all of this takes time before there is enough accomplishment to begin working. Frequently, when an academic degree is required, schooling can become boring. There are always prescribed subjects not needed for the work and you may not particularly want to take the time to pursue these subjects.

When you are older, schooling can make you impatient to get on with your life's work, particularly if it will take several years to finish — years that seem to take away from the work itself. For example, if you decide to be a lawyer or a doctor at age 30 or 40, it will take years of training before the work is even begun, not leaving many years left to actually do the work.

How do you pursue this kind of a vocation? How do you study when you are impatient to start the work? To say you need to learn patience and have the right attitude is not enough, and it certainly will not satisfy those feelings. In reality, the vocation chosen demands a lot of hard preparatory work for many years, and that reality can dampen your desire and enthusiasm to the extent that you give it up before the proper schooling is completed. This is unfortunate, but certainly understandable. What can you do to change this attitude and keep yourself totally involved, even on the dullest of schedules?

In order to have the needed enthusiasm, you must own your vocation. Owning your vocation means literally not only believing in it, not only wanting to do it, but also making it so much a part of your being that the question of not doing it — even in the midst of the most difficult times — will never arise. If you deeply believe in your destiny, then nothing and no one can interfere, no matter how difficult a vocation it is to accomplish, no matter how much hard work it may take to prepare yourself, and no matter who tries to affect it, including loved ones.

This type of deep conviction is what you need to develop, because it will give the stimulus to carry on enthusiastically under even the worst conditions. Look at some of the great artists who lived in dire poverty, with nothing but a deep love of painting. Many of them died unknown, but are recognized today as having given great beauty to the planet. Nothing and no one could make them give up painting. The same is true of many of the professions. Individuals with strong inner convictions that their work must be done are the ones who eventually cause change to happen around them and in the world itself. How many have lost their dream due to circumstance and a lack of inner belief in the chosen work? It is inner conviction that produces the strong desire and the energy needed to go forward.

When you have come to an understanding of your vocation, how do you develop the deep conviction that is so necessary? Practice the following visualization techniques and let your higher Self help you on your way.

Close your eyes and imagine yourself doing your work successfully in good surroundings. Experience this very clearly.

Next, connect with your higher Self[1] and ask:

---

[1]See the higher Self exercises, chapter 1, pp. 4-7.

Please help me feel or sense what it is like to be successfully doing my vocation.

Do this exercise and repeat it often until you really feel within yourself the joy of accomplishing your destined work. Even if the work seems far away, with little reality, imagine it clearly and with deep emotion, so as to really know what it would be like to do it. In the second exercise, connect with your higher Self, then ask:

Please show me all the blocks I will have to go through, if there are any, in order to fulfill my vocation.

Try to sense them clearly, write them down, make a list. Then take each one and look at it for deeper understanding. Put the block, whatever it is, in your heart and ask your higher Self:

Please show me the way I can best and most easily overcome this particular block.

For example, if one of your blocks is impatience, you may come to a realization, based on who you are, about the meaning of impatience itself. Your higher Self may show you some techniques you can do during the day to help you to overcome the attitude. Even before you encounter obstacles or blocks, by doing this exercise you will have a much better understanding of them, and it will be easier for you to go through them when they do occur.

These two exercises are helpful in conditioning you to believe in your life's work and to assist you in achieving it more easily. Along with this will come a deeper conviction, which will give you the enthusiasm you also need to have.

Enthusiasm is what sparks your energy. Never let anyone kill your enthusiasm. If someone tries to, avoid the person, no matter who it is, even if it is someone close to you. If one of your parents, for instance, is against you furthering your education, simply do not talk about it. Change the subject if the parent is negative. Remember, the work itself is difficult, and you need to have people around you who are not only enthusiastic about your doing it but who also believe in you.

Choose your friends and lovers wisely. This is so important for your growth. In turn, help those around you do their work by being, in a similar manner, enthusiastic about what they are doing. How much greater joy is there in all of this if you can simply believe in yourself and in others! This belief is very important. Without it the struggle is much greater.

Pursuing your vocation can be very hard work, but when it is right it will also be a lot of fun. The fun is in knowing the correct way to do it and in feeling a sense of accomplishment at all times. If you don't want to study something, think of the other aspects you love about it. Say to yourself, "I can do this because it is necessary for me to do the other," and always keep the goal in mind, knowing the goal will bring you happiness.

17

WHEN THE GOING GETS TOUGH

In the last few chapters many conditions are mentioned that affect doing and starting vocations. Let's suppose you know your vocation, but there are several reasons why you can't pursue it. For instance, you are married, have a family, and need to make enough money to support your loved ones. You can only work at your vocation in your spare time. You have completed the guidelines and have made a plan to follow which makes room for the work to begin.

Yet, even with guidelines, things happen to stop you. What if your spouse gets sick and you have to take on extra household chores, including taking care of the children? Naturally, your plan has to be put aside a while. In most cases, the vocation is neglected because of an emergency. Most people live with sudden emergencies as part of their normal routines. The man who is laying aside his plans to take care of his wife will have a sick child soon after, or a home emergency—the porch leaks when it rains. There is always something to prevent the plan from being followed.

Of course, when it comes down to realities, life is full of sudden happenings that always take up more time than you had allowed for. Try not to let yourself get caught in this kind of pattern. You can create the patterns yourself without being aware you are doing so. If a man's wife is sick, he, of course, has to nurture her; but caring for her and his children can be fitted into the plan. If he looks at his outline carefully and eliminates his personal needs and substitutes the needs of his wife and children, he can still have some time for his vocation work. It relates to priorities — what is most important. Naturally, the wife and children would come first but, certainly, the life's work should come next, not tennis, or movies, or reading the paper. Those things can go back into his plan when his wife is back to doing her part of the work.

Also, people often carelessly substitute something less important than the vocation work. This more trivial thing becomes part of the daily routine and, slowly, the other work becomes neglected. This is particularly the case when the life's work is tedious and requires extra effort. "Let's put it off" becomes the attitude, and before you know it the vocation work is being done less and less. It can be discouraging to realize how far we can get from the goal. The following example illustrates this situation.

> Rosalyn was a woman in her late 20s, full of energy and constantly on the go, immersed in all kinds of worthwhile projects. She was a volunteer in an association for peace and chaired a committee for another cultural organization. Though she worked full time, her evenings and weekends were spent in meetings and working for these different groups. The activities were her social life; all her friends were from these groups, as were the men she went out with, though they were few and far between. Getting married was not one of Rosalyn's priorities, and since she was always so busy there was no time to be lonely.

> She came to me because she was bored with her job. She had been a legal secretary for six or seven years and had no desire to go to college to further her career in business. She had thought about working full time for one of her organizations, but she

couldn't afford to live on the non-profit salary she would have made. Besides, the thing she liked most about her volunteer work was the friendships with her co-workers. The actual work itself she felt would also bore her if she had to do it full time.

She was surprised and very happy to find out that her vocation was to be a painter. She had dabbled in art as a teenager but had never taken it seriously. The fact that it would require extra training was fine with her. She enrolled in a drawing class at a local college and really enjoyed it, but she still continued her full load of volunteer work, which left little time for homework. Also, just staying at home, drawing, didn't fulfill her social needs; she wanted to be with people she knew and liked. However, the course was fun, and she did well in it.

After taking the drawing class for two years (the class was one night a week), Rosalyn found that her work was not developing in the way she had hoped. She added a second course in watercolors but still refused to do any work at home. After another year went by, with just a little improvement, she became discouraged and quit entirely. It was a waste of time, she felt, and she didn't want to waste time she could use elsewhere.

Unfortunately, Rosalyn had never committed herself to being an artist, never made art the priority. She had been unwilling to give up any outside activities or to look seriously at what she would have to do in order to fulfill her vocation.

Routine is the worse enemy. It impedes creativity. If Wednesday night is laundry night and you find yourself involved in a real creative project, to stop the creative work to do the laundry is jarring. And if you have a partner who demands that the laundry be done when it is supposed to be done, a fight can ensue if you say no, which will also break the momentum. It is better not to make such definite plans. Instead, keep it open. If it's your turn to do the laundry, decide it will be one of three nights, depending on what is happening with your work. As long as you do it within a few days and don't put it off too long, there should be no objection.

Unfortunately, we are all full of rigid patterns, taught to us by our parents. Let go of the rigid patterns. Go to the opposite extreme if you need to, in order to break away, but don't do it as an over-reaction. Change the pattern because you know it's too rigid and needs to be loosened up a bit. Never maintain a routine that hurts your creative flow. Look carefully at what you do and watch to see if the creative flow is being disturbed. If your energy level is down because you're doing something in a particular way, experiment. Try accomplishing the job in a different way. Develop another pattern, then change that one when it feels like it, too, is settling into a habit.

When you look at your vocation and start planning the work, again use your imagination to determine how you are going to tackle it. If your work requires a lot of studying and concentration, try different ways to learn the best method. Don't just automatically open a book and start reading. Look through the part you need to remember first, noting the illustrations, if there are any, and pick up a phrase or two. Then go to the beginning and start reading. The next time, you may want to vary the process. So try reading your notes and making cards to study, then looking for those key words in the text. Or try to memorize material with the use of tape recorders and video. And let your mind stay active during all these processes, assessing which way helps you the most. Select the best way and stay with it until you feel the energy failing again. Then begin experimenting again. You still might go back to an earlier way of doing it, but the experimenting will have reawakened your energies.

Stay tuned in to your body. How is it feeling? How do you experience your energy? If it is low, you may need to take a break. Go for a walk, or even do one of the other things on your list.

Often a spouse will interrupt you in your most creative moment. Don't get upset or angry, as it will interrupt the flow even more. Simply answer calmly and say you can talk later. Always be aware of your loved ones' feelings so he or she will not feel left out. There is a tendency in couples for one to listen and the other one to talk. The one who is talking will keep on and on and the other will tune out, which infuriates the talker. Try to balance a relationship with both communication and silence. Be honest about yourself and your needs, bearing in mind your partner also has needs. Try to fulfill those needs unless they become too demanding — then they need to be addressed by direct confrontation.

Never think anything has to be a certain way because you or your spouse have always done it that way. Be flexible. So often, rigidity sets in because of habits that make one feel secure — if everything is in the proper order, then everything will be all right. But how untrue this is, and how very easy it is to become victim to this type of attitude. Too many close their eyes to the horrors happening around them for fear of anything interrupting their own carefully planned lives.

Look at every task with new eyes, never see it the same way. Let your mind be fanciful, bringing fun into the mediocre. If your attitude is open and inquiring, then every routine will have its good points. You can be full of laughter, laughter that can be a catalyst for those around you. This keeps everyone happy. So always try to be light in manner and full of fun in your heart. When you convey this to others, it will make them see you positively and send you caring thoughts. These thoughts will help you in your work. The opposite can also happen. If you are negative to those around you, they will respond the same way and their thoughts will also affect your ability to do your work well.

Let go of the idea that everything is hard work. The person who feels this way often plays the martyr, making himself or herself miserable as well as affecting others with these feelings of being over-burdened. Let your attitude be one of alertness. Allow yourself the luxury of humor, the luxury of listening to beautiful music and the luxury of sending and receiving love. All these things will help you do your work well and bring you happiness.

18

OVERCOMING DIFFICULTIES
WITH THE NEW WAY

The new way refers to your new direction after you have discovered your vocation. Let's keep the word *new* because it denotes that there was an old way. The old way is what you had been doing. This new way can be full of the old way of doing things, which can sometimes cause problems, as it did in the following example.

> Ginny worked in a corporation for many years as a secretary. Though she had been a good student in high school, she had chosen not to go on to college and went directly to work. She hadn't anticipated working for very long, because she wanted to marry and have children. When Ginny was 22, she married and had two children. It was impossible to exist on her husband's salary alone, especially if they wanted a nice home. So, as soon as her children could go to day care, Ginny returned to work.
>
> She was a good secretary. It only took her a couple of years to reach the highest position possible as a secretary. Later, when she was in her early 30s, and tiring of the same routine, Ginny realized that to advance in her career it would be necessary to expand her education. Her company was willing to support her by paying half the tuition.

You can imagine how frightened she was about college! She had not studied for years and had never attended a university with huge classes taught in lecture halls. Fortunately, Ginny started off slowly, just taking a couple of night courses. Her major was business sciences, and she hoped one day to go for an MBA.

She tackled homework the way she had tackled her job. Being extremely well-organized, she spent a lot of hours developing a filing system to hold the information she was learning in the belief that if she kept everything in perfect order it would help her pass the course. But this caused her to lose the time and energy she needed for studying and memorization. As a result, she did poorly on her first tests.

Ginny realized her mistake. She knew she needed to learn sound study habits. Her school adviser assigned her a tutor, and when the second round of tests took place she fared much better.

Allocating time for doing things can be more time-consuming than if something is simply thought out and finished. In other words, before you spend time doing a particular task, think about the best and quickest way it can be accomplished and go the way of least complication. So often someone takes a simple task and spends hours thinking about doing it, instead of just doing it.

When a plan is necessary, again look for the best approach involving the least time spent, always keeping the goal in sight. If you find yourself spending hours on a project and nothing seems to be getting accomplished, then reassess the manner in which you're doing it and find out why nothing is happening.

Part of the learning process is discovering new ways to do things. Talk to others and ask them how they would go about doing something. There are many books available that describe different ways of being competent. Try one or two methods until you find what best suits you. Always be open to new ways of doing things and to the changes that take place.

If, for example, you are taking a course in college and need to know how to study for it, don't be afraid to go to the school advisers and get their opinions; also, you can learn from other students, those at the top of the class. Ask to spend an evening with one of them, to study together. This can teach you new methods. Never be afraid to ask for advice or feel it is beneath you to ask someone younger for help.

The same is true if you are working at a new type of job. If there has been little job training, you may need to ask for help from colleagues or your supervisor. It's important to learn the right way from the beginning. Don't ever feel unworthy if you're not knowledgeable. Everyone needs to learn at the beginning, and a good employer will help you and not expect you to do things perfectly at the outset. No matter how difficult a task or job may seem, there is always someone who has done it before you. If that individual still works for the company don't be afraid to ask for help. If the person has left the company, you can still connect by doing the following exercise:

Connect with your heart. Visualize or sense the person who had your job before you. (If you know what he or she looks like, try to get the image, otherwise imagine a body. The face can be blank or indistinguishable.)

Experience a light flowing from your heart to the person's heart and say:

Please send me all the knowledge you have about how to do my job successfully.

It is sometimes a burden to have to relearn ways of doing things. A habit is very hard to break. But this same habit, while working for you in one way, can really impede you in another as you can see from the example that follows.

Bill was a competent manager. He had climbed the ladder very quickly and was in a top position in a middle-sized company that manufactured electronic equipment. His style of working was the typical vertical, hierarchical method: he made the decisions and delegated the work. Each worker was accountable to him directly. It was fast and easy for the type of production involved. The only thing Bill didn't like about his job was the pay scale. He had reached the limit. To make more he would have to change jobs.

His next position was with a leading Fortune 500 company as head of a product group with a slightly larger staff than the one he had worked with before. The company gave him an operations manual and some brief training in its methodology. It was a radically different system; the shift was to group work. At every level the professionals would meet as a group and arrive at a consensus in making decisions. Part of Bill's job was to participate, monitor the group, and examine the creative output in terms of viability.

He also was part of a group comprising the managers of all the product lines whose purpose was to share ideas and information on developments within the departments. If there were problems, this was the place to air them and get feedback.

To say the job was a challenge would be an understatement. Not only did Bill need to learn everything about his product line, he also had to revise his managerial style. Working in a group was a new, difficult experience for him. When he fell back into his old style of giving orders, which he did often, the reaction from his workers was hostile. Sharing information and problems was also new to him, and he was reluctant to do so.

One of the other managers who had befriended him then suggested a school where Bill could learn more about some of the new structural techniques businesses were using. He enrolled in some courses in progressive management styles and, though he made quite a few blunders, he learned quickly and was able to keep his job.

No one way is perfect or set. We must all take and develop what is right for us. When an individual is stuck in one way being the only way, then that individual will cease to grow spiritually. Even when accomplishing the vocation, the individual will develop such a rigid way of doing things that this personality trait will be carried to the next life or lives.

Be flexible and be aware of all the changes around you, the changes that affect what you are doing either positively or negatively. If it is the latter, learn to quickly change yourself, so as to negate any adverse effects. And open your awareness by harmonizing your heart and mind so that they work together.

19

Who Will Help You and Who Will Not

Often when you make a major life change, friends are not supportive. In fact, they may even try to dissuade you from pursuing the new work. This happens because the friend is sometimes also wanting a change but doesn't have the courage or the energy to make it happen. Such a person resents anyone who is striving in a new direction.

It may be necessary to let go of some of your old friends if this happens. If you are struggling to learn something new and you have people around who are not only unhelpful but downright negative about what you're doing, then you need to really look at each and every one and decide if each is truly a friend. A true friend should be supportive.

It is also possible that a negative friend may be feeling fearful of being deserted by you. This can be unconscious. The friend may be reacting to your learning new things beyond the friend's understanding. The fear is that the more you learn the more distant you will become and the more you will not need that friendship.

It's important here to find out what the friend is feeling and not just go by what is said. Sometimes the friend will be hurtful and sarcastic, other times quiet and cold. Be aware of how the friend must be feeling, how threatening it must be to see someone you love go off in a direction you cannot understand or get enthusiastic about.

Remember, this friend will more often than not deny the truth. Telling you about feeling a loss because you are branching out into new things will not help the situation. More than likely, the friend will deny such feelings and certainly won't want you to think jealousy is involved. The truth might well be that the friend *is* jealous and does not want you to be superior in any way because then you may leave and find new friends.

So many dreams that could have happened are destroyed by would-be friends who will say you're crazy to spend all your time on something that may or not be successful.

If you ask your family to be supportive, you can do the same with your friends. The difference is, your family is usually karmic, and most people are bound by karma to interact. You generally keep your family, no matter what happens; but you don't have to keep your friends. Look at each carefully and determine how you really feel. Is each a friendship in which you help one another, or has it stayed the same from the beginning? Also, recognize if someone is afraid of losing you, and talk about it openly, making certain all the feelings are discussed. You may want to keep your friends, but if they are not supportive during this time of transition, then you might need to re-evaluate the relationships.

It is important to understand how the energy around you needs to breathe. Breathing is the flow of prana into the physical body from your subtle body and out to the work you are doing. The more concentrated the work, the more energy is able to flow freely. Negative energy directed toward you will be eliminated by your positive force, but not without your paying the price of your energy being lessened. This is why you need to avoid negative thinking and negative interchanges.

If friends are negative because of their own personal problems, it will not affect your energy. You can help them by sending them love from the heart. This energy is constantly renewed. It is only when they start to bring you into their problems that you should question the intent. The following story illustrates this.

William and Ted were buddies all through their teens, even going to the same college to be together. After graduation they moved to the big city, got jobs, shared an apartment, and settled into living the typical bachelor life.

Ted was good-looking, sociable, and loved the night life that the city offered in abundance. Women flocked to him and he moved through one affair after another as if losing count were a goal. William, on the other hand, was shy and introverted. He soon tired of partying every night, getting no sleep, and having Ted pick his bed partners, each guaranteed to perform "the best."

William was also unhappy with the work he was doing, which is why he had come to me for help. His vocation turned out to be law, a profession he had never thought about, but which now made him feel excited and enthusiastic.

He quit his job, took out a few loans and was accepted by a leading law college in the city. In the beginning he kept the apartment with Ted, but the frequent parties interfered with his studies, and Ted didn't seem to understand that he needed quiet in order to study. William finally moved to a small room near campus.

Losing his lifelong companion was difficult for Ted. He found that going out was no fun unless William was along — having him there had made a difference! So he constantly telephoned William, berating him with, "What kind of friend are you? Why don't you have more time to see me?" and "How can you

work all day and night? It must be very boring!"
and "Look what you're missing. There've been some
great parties" and "You're never any fun anymore."

William tried talking to him but it was no use, he
just didn't understand. Ted would shout and scream
at him or get drunk and call him in a rage; he was
unable to look at his fears and insecurities. William
had been the strong, silent one, the person Ted knew
would always be there. When he wasn't, it was dev-
astating. The friendship survived only because William convinced Ted to go into therapy, which helped
him see some of these things for himself.

Remember the friend who is helpful. See more of him because his belief in you will enhance your energy. Never lose
sight of anyone like this. Such a friendship is wonderful to
have. Let your discrimination tell you when a person is sincerely interested and supportive.

It is also wise to keep your friends apart from your work.
Don't talk about it to them, as talking enthusiastically may
bring up their fears. Instead, enjoy their company in exactly
the same way you did before. This will help them feel you are
still the same person and that what you are doing on the side
won't hurt or change you. Make them aware you care, though
you have less time to see them. Don't hesitate to express your
love for them. If you say it openly, it will be remembered later
on. You should also let your friends know how much you
have to do in order to be successful; then they will not expect
you to be around all the time.

Never be afraid to cut off a relationship—no matter how
old it is—if the friend is demanding, negative or sarcastic
about what you're doing. This kind of person will probably
always stay this way, no matter what is happening. The reason
a friend is competitive is because that friend relates too personally to what you're doing, and if it doesn't feel right for
the friend, the belief is that it can't be right for you. Let go. If

you do, your friend may realize how such behavior is affecting you and make amends.

If you have negative friends you really love and don't want to lose, then simply see less of them for the time being. Remember to first talk to people and explain how you feel. Only if there is no understanding should you break off a relationship.

Never keep a friend because you feel pity or sympathy. Neither is a good basis for friendship. The person who clings to you is also someone you need to gently let go of. Attachment only brings karma and karmic ramifications. If you are attracted to someone, remember to discern whether this is a relationship from a past life and follow your intuition accordingly. Choose your friends carefully, looking for positive-mindedness, enthusiasm, and genuine love.

20

Using Your Higher Self
While You Work

When you begin working toward achieving your vocation, the difficulties and obstacles will be easy to overcome if you consciously utilize the higher Self. Activating it as fully as possible is very important. Often, people fail at their work because they fear attempting to go beyond personal limits. Daring is as much a part of the higher Self as is right-mindedness.

Right-mindedness is the result of linking your heart and mind to the mind of your higher Self, which is connected to the higher forces in the universe. These forces are in harmony with the higher Self and impress wisdom into it. Therefore, activating the higher Self will help you to be tuned in to the cosmos and to the vibrations around you produced by nature itself. Being one with nature means to have knowledge far beyond the limits of the physical body.

Now, stop for a minute, close your eyes, and using one of the higher Self exercises,[1] ask your higher Self:

What do I need to do to consciously be one with you while I am working?

Try to hear or feel something. Each person has a different psychic makeup, so it's best to ask your higher Self for the right exercise for you to do. Ask:

---

[1]See the higher Self exercises, chapter 1, pp. 4-7.

Please show or let me feel a specific exercise I can do that will help in the process of becoming one with you. At another time, connect with the higher Self and ask:

Please show or let me sense a symbol that represents you.

When you see a symbol, take time to draw it, frame it, and hang it over your work area. Each time you work, link your heart with the higher Self, visualize the symbol, imagine placing it in your heart and ask to be totally one with the higher Self.

When you find yourself stuck for any reason, close your eyes and think of the symbol, holding it in focus over whatever is causing you trouble. This is helpful to do during examinations and tests, in general.

Practice these exercises every day for at least 15 minutes. Also, try to remember while you are doing routine work to link with the higher Self, and It will make it easier. The more you practice using the higher Self, the more you will find yourself achieving things you could not do before. Knowledge is for all, but it requires an effort of will to strive to find it. The higher Self contains the answer to every existing question. To realize how it works is to understand nature itself, and with that understanding comes a deeper perception of yourself, who you are, and your purpose on the planet.

All of the unknowns in life can be known if you develop the power to become one with the higher Self. All of humanity will someday develop these abilities. For some it will take millions of years, for others only a short time. It depends on each person's evolutionary path and where on the path that individual is at a given time. The way to accelerate the process is to consciously work with the higher Self. Use It in everything you do, be one with It when you relate to others, feel It in your heart when you see someone in need, know It in your mind when you sense the right way to do something. Be one with It during your work so you can be more effective and efficient.

Naturally, such an ability requires time to develop; it can't be done overnight. Also, there will be times when you cannot contact the higher Self. Usually this is because the lower nature is frightened and bringing up fears in you — fears that are keeping you from being one with the higher Self. At such times, try to look impersonally at what it is you fear. If the fear is very strong, you may want to talk to someone or get help. If it is too scary, try dissipating it by getting more rest, and when you're feeling better, ask your higher Self for help in understanding the fear and how to best overcome it.

The answers to all questions lie within you. Getting them takes concentration and an inner belief that you will understand someday. Your own higher Self will show you this when it is right to know. Never force knowing. Let it come naturally, trusting that it will be understood when your consciousness is ready to know it.

If there is a hidden trauma from the past, it will come out; but, again, do not force it. Let your higher Self be the one to bring it into consciousness. Otherwise, you can be hurt emotionally. Everything has its proper pace and way. Trust in this, and in your higher Self, and if you believe in any of the higher Beings,[2] then link with the one you feel closest to and trust that you will be helped.

---

[2]Jesus, Moses, Buddha, Mohammed — any of the Masters of the White Brotherhood, etc.

21

WHY THIS PARTICULAR WORK?

Doing your vocation will happen when you have a real understanding about its nature and why a particular vocation should be done in a specific lifetime. I have discussed in previous chapters that fulfilling your life's work will help in your personal evolution. Doing the vocation will propel you onward in the right way. If you don't do your vocation, you will have to return at another time to do that precise task, to complete a cycle in order to go forward into another. The more times you are successful in doing your vocation, the faster you will evolve.

To always be successful is rare, but as you grow spiritually you will have a better understanding and therefore more chance to accomplish the work and go onward. If you are very aware of your vocation and the reason for it, you have a much better chance of completing it.

If you understand the reason, you will not only do the work, but will also become deeply involved in it. Understanding comes from looking at your history in terms of lifetimes. If you are to be an artist and have been an artist in the past, there may be something not accomplished or completed that is drawing you back to that vocation. Therefore, it is important to find out what the something is, so as to be certain to achieve it in this lifetime. If, instead, you are to be an artist because art has never been done before and the experience is needed in the consciousness, then it is important to look at everything in the field of art to be certain to choose the area in which success is most likely. Remember, it is not worldly success, but an inner feeling of accomplishment that is meaningful. This way, when you leave the body at death, you don't have to repeat the vocation.

Often, someone will want to do a particular vocation because it was so gratifying in a past life that there is an inner need to continue it. This type of individual might in fact choose the same vocation several times, just because of those inner desires. It is important to know this in order to let go at last and move on to another profession. Such a person is frequently in the arts and sciences, creative fields that pull in the higher energies and affect the soul. The spirit's inner knowledge of this is a factor when someone chooses one of these areas to continue working in. Realizing this can release the need and help the person select, instead, a work that will directly enhance experience. Otherwise, there can be stagnation.

To come to a better understanding of what your particular relationship is to your vocation, you would be wise to consult your higher Self, because It is aware of everything you have done before and can relate parts of the experience to you. Connect with your higher Self[1] and ask:

> *Please tell or show me if I have a particular relationship to my vocation.*

Also ask:

> *Have I done this work before?*

If the answer is yes, then ask:

> *Please show me more about this past relationship. How does it relate to the present work?*

---

[1]See the higher Self exercises, chapter 1, pp. 4-7.

Tell or show me more that can help me do the present work.

It is important that you keep asking the higher Self to let you experience more. It will eventually start to send you indications, either directly in meditation or in dreams, but you must keep asking on a regular basis until you have been told. Everything is within you, and it will come out as long as you persist in asking. Repetition is important here, as it sends the same vibratory energy over and over again.

When there are resistances to knowing about the relationship, it will take longer to get an answer, but don't be discouraged. Remember, the answer is within you and it is your right to know. Let the higher Self overcome your fears and obstacles.

22

Tuning In Without Dropping Out

When you are going through the period of training needed to accomplish your vocation, you may become so preoccupied with the work you forget your friends and loved ones. You simply don't think about them. If they are understanding, they will realize you are very busy and therefore have little time for them. If they are very sensitive, they may feel you are neglecting them purposely, and may even feel you have abandoned them.

What you need to realize is that many people don't understand what it's like to be totally immersed in something — so immersed there is no other awareness. Such concentration comes when you are finally working at your vocation and feeling the satisfaction of that. People generally work 9 to 5 and come home to relax. To continue working after those hours daily would make some feel they were being mis-used by their employers. As a result, to use leisure time to pursue another profession would be considered crazy by some.

Unfortunately, many believe that neglecting those you know for your career means you no longer care. If you say this isn't true, that you still care, some will feel you are lying. Such an attitude is hard to deal with. How do you explain the truth without hurting feelings or causing skepticism? Often, it's impossible. Even the person you love the most may be one of those people, and so you may lose that person. Because the work is time-consuming, it not only takes you physically away but also your concentration can become so intense you can't think of anything else. As a result, you may only talk about the work, neglecting to even try to find out how a friend is feeling. How many relationships break up because one person is totally self-centered!

Your closest friend can, perhaps, be the best one to talk to your other friends. This means you have to convince that friend of your sincerity and then ask for help in convincing the others. Usually there is a loved one who is close enough to understand, who will be happy to help. If, instead, this person is one of those who is having trouble with you, then choose someone else, someone who is more objective and understanding. Also, if you can, it's good to select someone who has gone through intensive work and knows how important and fulfilling it is. Ask the person to share this experience, and what feelings it elicited.

In this manner, the friend can compare this experience with what is happening to you and answer questions others may feel uncomfortable in asking you. The best approach would be to ask directly what the friend feels about your being busy all the time. This is a good way to get into the topic. The following case demonstrates this point.

Lisa was back in college studying journalism. She worked during the day and was taking three courses at night, with a heavy load of homework. This took a heavy toll on her social life. Since school was her priority, she had limited seeing friends and dating.

Helen and Lois were her two closest girlfriends. The three had been inseparable, doing everything and going everywhere together. But no more. Now she had to limit doing things with them. Her friends understood; or at least she thought they did. She had made a point of talking to them about how she felt — she really wanted to be with them more, but for now her career was very important and she needed to pursue it.

Helen seemed to understand, but Lois would be quiet and appear hurt when Lisa refused an invitation to go out. Lisa kept telling Lois not to take it personally, that she really valued her friendship. But it didn't work. Because Lois's surly attitude became such a problem to be around, Lisa found herself avoiding her more and more and spending her spare time with Helen or other friends.

Helen was caught in the middle, listening to complaints from both. When it became too much, she decided to intervene. One night she cornered Lois and got her to really talk about her feelings concerning Lisa. Lois said she basically felt abandoned by Lisa, and as they talked it became obvious to Helen that Lois's insecurities were based on her relationship with an older sister she adored. The two had been very close as children, but when the sister started dating, she'd stopped having anything to do with Lois.

Lois was feeling this desertion again, and even though she knew Lisa's preoccupation was with school work, she couldn't help feeling hurt. She also felt that if she told Lisa of her fears of losing the friendship, Lisa would think she was being neurotic. That had been her sister's reaction when she'd complained about never seeing her anymore. Helen helped Lois to share her feelings with Lisa, and it smoothed the way to a more mature relationship.

When you live with someone who doesn't understand, try another approach. Ask the person to be with you while you are studying. Say you miss the conversation and that it would make you feel better to know the person is in the same room.

Ask the person to read a book or even take a nap in the same area. Though the person may not want to do this, preferring a more active recreation, by simply asking you are saying you still care.

Taking a break to have a drink and five minutes of conversation or the time to give a friend an embrace can mean the difference between keeping a relationship or losing it. The friend knows you are busy, sees it clearly, but still may feel that your work is more important. Expressing love always helps.

There will also be times when you really need to be alone. When even the presence of another will be a distraction, and you know you can't continue unless you are alone. Talking about this is important and is usually sufficient for most couples. But if a spouse or loved one still feels left out and hurt about your needing to be alone, plan to take a walk at a time when the loved one is busy or out. Disappear in your car and drive to a quiet place where you can be alone. Don't talk about it, just do it. If asked later where you've been, just say you felt the need for some fresh air. Next time, make a point of doing the same thing — getting some fresh air — but with the loved one along. Find yourself a private place where you can sit, without too many people around, or a wooded place where you can talk.

Those of you who live alone need to do the opposite at times. No matter now much work you have to do, find time to see a friend, even if it's only for half an hour. Make the time to have dinner with someone, or telephone a friend during a few minutes' break. Some people won't do this. They break their ties and bury themselves in their work and are happy. If the work is boring, you will take breaks, but when you are feeling the joy of accomplishment, this is sometimes hard to do. Force yourself, because you need the balance of relationships.

Never deny loved ones time if they are needing you. Try to be consciously aware of when need is need and not someone being demanding. If it is the latter, deal with it by being open in your feelings. Too often, the demanding one will deny feelings of abandonment. Try to help that person be aware of the unconscious needs. If the demands are never-ending and you are not left alone, try separating for a short time, going away for a few days, and make it clear why you are going. This way the loved one will take what you are saying seriously.

When a loved one is very close and has spent a long time with you, sharing everything and being there when you are needy, it may hurt to see you happy without being a part of it. Again, reassure with attention as much as possible. Try being affectionate, even if you have not been that way before. A warm hug can make all the difference. Make certain to talk about your work without making it the only subject of conversation. Try to be interested in everything your loved one is doing and ask for details about things you may have missed because of work.

Also talk about your future together and how you will both benefit from the work you are learning. This then becomes something you can both strive for. The future is always brightest when people who love each other help each other find their dreams.

23

STAYING IN TOUCH WITH YOUR INTENTIONS

Often, when you are working fully at your vocation and are feeling a sense of accomplishment, blocks will come up in the work. These blocks or difficulties can arise because there are still fears within that relate to successfully accomplishing the work. These fears can sometimes bring confusion and distrust concerning the vocation.

The inner critic (which most people have) will at this time relay all kinds of messages to the consciousness, mainly about not being good enough, and questioning the validity of the work and whether it really is necessary. This can strongly affect your sense of accomplishment. Often, too, such fears will cast doubt on the vocation itself. Did I really understand this correctly? Maybe I was mistaken and this is really not my vocation and all this work is for nothing?

It's amazing how one day you can be doing very well and feeling real joy about your work, and the next day you wake up with a sense of total failure, with negative feelings about everything so far accomplished. Such feelings can arise because you have achieved a true state of oneness with the vocation, which causes the opposite to arise out of the unconscious to try to influence in the other direction. When the positive is happening, it attracts the opposite, the negative. This pull between opposing poles continues until you realize where both are coming from and integrate them into what Buddha called the "middle way." This integration allows freedom and expansion. There is no longer the pressure of the negative or the idealism of the positive. There is, instead, a way of flowing with all that happens in its natural course. Then you will feel no need to struggle to achieve your goal. It will happen when it is meant to happen.

This last phase brings you a true sense of meaning and purpose. It is the synthesis that changes and brings the higher Self into conscious reality. Of course, the balance can go off under pressure and outside influences, but it will be easily restored and the course resumed. The following case shows how this might happen.

> When Jessica discovered her vocation was to be in politics, she was thrilled. She envisioned herself becoming the first woman president! Plunging in with incredible vigor, she had no trouble getting a law degree and landed a job working in the mayor's office. Her career was a bold arrow pointing straight ahead.

> The evening hours were spent at the party's local office, where she made herself known by championing underdog causes. Soon, however, some of the inherent corruption of party politics became visible and started blocking her efforts. She vehemently fought for what she thought was right and just, but with no satisfaction. Any favor had a lot of strings attached.

> Depression set in. Everything was wrong—the system, and of course herself—she wasn't good enough to make herself heard. Her career became a monstrous joke. She quit everything except her job, which would pay the rent until she could decide what to do with her life.

> Jessica believed that if she did her best the system would always work. But her belief system was so

idealistic that at the first touch of reality it fell, broken in pieces. Nothing was any good, then. There was no hope.

It took time, and a good bit of counseling, for Jessica to put the pieces back together into a more realistic package. No longer was she naive in believing right action always produces right results. Instead, little by little, she was able to see how doing the right thing can make a difference, even if it can't completely change things.

Jessica rejoined the party, this time choosing to fight for things she really felt had a chance of succeeding. She no longer championed all the underdogs, but carefully chose those that made sense in the community. When last heard of, she was making a good name for herself as a caring liberal with values. Becoming the first woman president may still be Jessica's goal, but it no longer rings with idealism.

Much of what happens in your life depends on balancing the opposites. There are many ways and paths to finding this balance within. It is up to you to know the best way. Finding the best way takes time and the experience of life itself.

During the pursuit of your vocation, you will more than likely confront the struggle of right action versus indecisiveness, the inability to do what is needed and, most of all, the inability to perform. Each will require a struggle if you are to regain the focus needed to go on. Each will come from the inner you, afraid to face the responsibility right action brings. To understand this requires looking at yourself through the eyes of your higher Self. Your higher Self knows who you really are and can give you the understanding you need for the struggle. Always connect with It during times of doubt and negativity. Connect through the heart, and allow It to help you. Realize this is the part of you that will bring about the needed balance.

Remember that the goal of achieving your vocation is the potential you bring into this lifetime with you. The goal can be achieved, as long as you believe nothing can stop your reaching it. Your higher Self will help you make it real.

When you go through moments of discouragement, connect with your higher Self[1] and ask:

Please help me to understand why I'm feeling discouraged.

When you have a better understanding of why, then ask:

Please show me what I need to do to overcome this feeling. Keep working with it and the discouragement will drop away.

So often people think of themselves as having no way to change their lives, lives frequently full of misery. They are bound in karma they cannot get out of. Yet, within each and every one of us is a higher Self ready to help break the bonds so we can create new and better realities.

---

[1]See the higher Self exercises, chapter 1, pp. 4-7.

24

Working with Past Lives

A way to help fulfill your vocation is to consciously utilize everything in your heart chalice that has access to the knowledge of previous lives. If you know those lives, it helps to bring forth some of the characteristics you had before and understand characteristics you have now. Sometimes the characteristics can be negative, so it's good to understand the life and what went wrong if this is the case. There will also be positive characteristics you need to re-own — characteristics that can help you in the work you're doing now.

Finding out about past lifetimes is a process. It should never be forced. Force will interfere with the natural process. Knowledge of a past life can be hurtful if the consciousness is not ready to look at it. One word of warning: there are some people who become very involved with knowing past lives. Some use them as a form of escape. A person may get caught up in feeling a past life is more important than the current one and may literally live in the past instead of working on the present personality. Also, having a famous past life can be used for spiritual one-upmanship. This is why any kind of forcing of the memory of a past life can be dangerous. Knowing the past is strictly to help one see old characteristics — nothing more — and should not be indulged in.

Certainly, the most recent past lifetime will bring you the strongest characteristics, and since your latest past life often reflects capabilities from earlier lifetimes, it is even more important to know it so as to draw upon those traits. If, for instance, you were a painter in the most recent past life, you may have the desire to paint in this life, though your vocation is to do other things. It would be all right in this case to pursue painting as a hobby, as long as it doesn't interfere with the vocation.

It is also important to know the most recent past life because it will reveal characteristics you may not be aware of. Some of these characteristics will help you or will hold you back. If, for example, your vocation in this life is to be a doctor and in your most recent past life you were a painter, you may find yourself having difficulty using your logical (often called left) brain. The intuitive (right brain) would be more developed given the past experience. It would now be better for you to work with both at the same time. If you are studying for a test that requires a lot of memorizing, your mind may be wandering, or you may feel fatigued from all the work. If so, take a moment to do a visualization. See yourself working as a doctor. See it clearly and let yourself experience how it feels. Then continue to study. This will help you use your intuition when you take the exam. Too much use of one side of the brain and not enough of the other will cause an imbalance and affect your results.

Many times in past lives you experienced love and had love relationships. It's good to see those relationships, to feel you had them, particularly if you aren't married now. If in the last life you experienced a loving marriage, you may long for such a relationship again. Such a longing can interfere with your achieving your vocation. So it is best to see the past, feel how it felt, and know you had it and that you can have it again when you know you are ready. Too often, people get married too soon because of the most recent life. An early marriage can also hurt one's career. The reason it is important to know all these things is so you can really understand yourself better. Only then will you be able to do your vocation freely.

Despite the barriers, knowing you did well in the past will help you achieve your vocation now. You have to look at the important occurrences and determine if they left deep impressions on your psyche. You must realize that all experiences are within you and if, for example, you had a recent past life experience of hurt and rejection, you will be overly sensitive to rejection in this life and can even believe it's happening to you when it's not.

When seeing a past life, try to look at the positive parts first and know them well before looking at the negative. So often a person sees the negative and feels the life was all negative. This is simply not true. A life is never all negative or all positive. Remember, balance is crucial. Even the high yogis have negative traits they are carefully watching and controlling.

When you are trying to discover a past lifetime, it is important to let it unfold intuitively by connecting with your higher Self[1] and asking:

If it will help me, please let me experience a past life that affects or is in any way connected to my present life's work.

You may want to draw how you looked. Close your eyes and ask the higher Self:

Please direct my drawing so that it resembles the way I looked in my past lifetime. Then just let your hand draw your face.

The main thing is to sense or feel the lifetime, because then you can understand your vocation from another perspective. If it is to be an actress, and in your last life you were a recluse, you will find it difficult to be before an audience. Knowing the past lifetime can release fears and help you to develop spiritually.

---

[1]See the higher Self exercises, chapter 1, pp. 4-7.

An individual who does not believe in reincarnation will not be able to pick up on past lifetimes. Disbelief will block this. Working with the higher Self will help such an individual recall what is needed from the unconscious.

As you contact your higher Self, you will become aware of characteristics you need to work on. Often these characteristics will change and develop as they are incorporated into consciousness, thereby making you stronger. For instance, if you were a statesman in your last life and died at a young age, it would leave you with a feeling of loss and may attract you back to that same field. This feeling of loss may in turn cause you to feel anguish and keep you from applying yourself to the work. You may want to have fun and play with friends, instead. But if you're aware of the reason for this, you can easily overcome such a tendency and begin to utilize the knowledge you gained in earlier lives, which will be a strong base for your further development.

25

With a Clear Mind and Dedication

Working to discover your vocation is the first step toward accomplishing your goal. Be careful not to rush that step. It is important to be certain you know what the vocation is. So even if it takes you a year or more, be patient. Let your higher Self guide you along the way.

The work itself is the easiest part, because it is work you want to do. Sometimes it is necessary to study other things that won't be as easy because they don't relate directly to the vocation. Also, be careful not to overwork yourself. Give yourself the time you need to accomplish the other things. It's better to start slowly and add on as you go along.

For those of you who need to return to school, do so without fear and without feeling out of place among the younger students. Keep your goal in mind when you experience difficulties, and remember to ask your higher Self for help.

Acknowledge and work with the higher Self on a daily basis. If you don't see or feel It at first, don't be discouraged. Continue consciously working with It and you will get results. Try experiencing It within, and when something you do comes out well, acknowledge the higher Self's part in that. You already use It much more than you are aware of in your daily life. When you help others, acknowledge that the need to do so comes from your higher Self. When you feel compassion, realize it comes through the heart from the higher Self.

Know that your higher Self is part of you and that you can become one with It, so that you *are* your higher Self most of the time.

If you feel negative and have difficulty getting in touch with the higher Self, link with your heart and ask for help from any of the higher Beings you may believe in — Jesus, Buddha, Moses, etc. If you are an atheist and feel uncomfortable doing this, link your heart to something that inspires you. Try to sense that beauty in you. Beauty is always a path to the higher Self.

Let your spirit come into your consciousness. Feel It opening and expanding within you and believe in yourself — in your higher Self and in your conscious self. Trust in the abilities you acquired before this life and in this life. Remember, you have accomplished many things in many different fields of endeavor. Don't be afraid to let these accomplishments come forth.

When you finally start to work on your vocation, having given yourself time to be sure you now know what it is, make a plan for how you will reach your goal. Make the plan simple, with time lines. This year you will begin this and that. Next year you will continue with this and start that. Include those things you really enjoy doing, and remember it is fun to work on your vocation. Even if it will require a lot of hard work, it can still be fun. If you feel this way, it will make the work easier.

Let your higher Self guide you along the way. Keep It in your awareness so you are always open to suggestions and criticisms. Be impersonal about everything you do, because non-attachment will certainly give you the best perspective of what is happening.

Let yourself feel everything, particularly the joy of accomplishing something that was hard to do. Acknowledge that you did well and when you are given help, which might come in various forms, acknowledge its source.

Know that you are starting on a new path that will lead you to your goal in this life. There may be obstacles along the way, but they will only make you stronger on the climb upward. For some, overcoming the obstacles may not require more than a simple step. For others it may require psychological work. Just keep the goal in mind and you will succeed. Remember, time is not as important as reaching the goal itself.

Don't let anyone talk you out of your dream. Be aware that the dream should be in your heart and not shared with those who are negative or skeptical. If your vocation is to do what some people think is inconceivable, don't listen to them. Realize that a far-reaching goal will take longer to achieve. Keep the goal of accomplishing your vocation in your heart. Ask your higher Self to show you a symbol that represents your goal. Know it and hold it before you during times of doubt.

Remember to be who you are — the *real* you — which is comprised of many aspects from many lifetimes. Choose positive characteristics and reawaken them. Look at apparent negative ones and try to transmute them. Build a link with your higher Self that is solid, and you will most certainly achieve your goal.

Don't forget you are part of nature, that your subtle body is within you and needs to fulfill itself as well. Synthesize all three — the subtle, the higher Self and the conscious self — and you will be operating in harmony with nature.

You are nature, remember that. Feel its power. Never separate yourself from its source. The food of the spirit is the nurturer of the three parts. This nourishment is the energy you need to accomplish your vocation. Feel it flow through you and, most of all, be happy, for happiness is the basis of all endeavors. Without it the work is cumbersome and unfulfilling; with it the work, even when it's most difficult, will flow smoothly.

Finally, be happy, and know that true happiness comes from within your own heart. Keep your heart open to all things, keep your heart loving to all people, and you will know the right way to accomplish your vocation.

When Nanette Hucknall was 28 years old, she took 72 hours of testing to find out what her aptitudes were. At the time, she was an advertising art director with a budding career, yet felt discontented and unfulfilled. The tests didn't help her discover her true vocation. This was only accomplished through many years of inner searching.

Combining her knowledge of eastern philosophy and psychology, Ms. Hucknall has developed a method to guide others in finding their true vocations. She is currently a partner in "Human Systems Design," consultants who specialize in psychological and systems approaches to personal and organizational transformation. She and her partners have designed and presented workshops and seminars internationally, some of which are "Balancing the Masculine and Feminine," "Developing the Intuition," "Beyond Image: Harmonizing the Inner and Outer Woman," and "Finding Your Work."

Ms. Hucknall has a B.F.A. from Cooper Union, and has trained in Psychosynthesis, a transpersonal psychology that uses experiential methodology in working with people. She has been a disciple in Agni Yoga for twenty-two years and has brought this knowledge and discipline to her work.